Praise for When the Clouds Come

"Drew's personality and enthusiasm resonate in every chapter of this fascinating new book. His curious approach looks at new perspectives, provokes a different way of thinking and stimulates meaningful conversation. Having worked with Drew on a range of different projects, I always find myself energised by his positive approach to business, leadership and life in general. I have no doubt this book will instill that same positive energy for its readers."
—Stuart Pearce MBE and Football Icon

"Up until now, there hasn't been a manual out there to help you lead through a truly unprecedented period like we currently face, but this book does exactly that! Personally, there is no one else I'd rather have to guide me through the tough times that we all inevitably encounter. I believe this book captures the magic of Drew brilliantly and will inspire all those who read it to look at life differently."
—Dave Capper: CEO, Westfield Health

"I would wholeheartedly recommend that you read this book to help build your strength and optimism and to understand that that the choices we make CAN make everything better. Drew is one of the few people I've met who can help me think through ways of dealing with the constant uncertainty we all experience in life. This book really is an essential companion for the world in which we currently live."
—Sophie Devonshire: CEO,
The Marketing Society

WHEN THE CLOUDS COME

DEALING WITH DIFFICULTIES, FACING YOUR FEARS, AND OVERCOMING OBSTACLES

DREW POVEY

WITH SAM DRAPER

CAPSTONE
A Wiley Brand

Registered office

John Wiley & Sons, Inc., 111 River Street, Hoboken, NJ 07030, USA
John Wiley & Sons Ltd, The Atrium, Southern Gate, Chichester, West Sussex, PO19 8SQ, United Kingdom

Editorial Office

John Wiley & Sons Ltd, The Atrium, Southern Gate, Chichester, West Sussex, PO19 8SQ, United Kingdom

For details of our global editorial offices, customer services, and more information about Wiley products visit us at www.wiley.com.

Wiley also publishes its books in a variety of electronic formats and by print-on-demand. Some content that appears in standard print versions of this book may not be available in other formats.

Library of Congress Cataloging-in-Publication Data is Available:

ISBN 9780857089175 (paperback)
ISBN 9780857089182 (ePub)
ISBN 9780857089199 (ePDF)

Cover Design: Wiley
Cover Image: © WindNoise/Shutterstock

SKY98198AAE-3E8A-4FC4-B117-24FE72DE9EFB_032422

Contents

Introduction

I think some people write books because it's their lifelong ambition, others because they think it's a business opening. I think people write books for a myriad of different reasons. For me it's always about, 'Can you put something out into the world that is going to make a difference?' That's it.

People normally write books because they're passionate about whatever their message is, or information they are parting with. Let's be honest, it's not that easy. It's quite a long and drawn-out process – well it is certainly that way for me. I wanted to write this book because I'm limited on the number of people I can share my thoughts and ideas with day to day, and I wanted to get those ideas down so that I can hopefully provide others, whom I wouldn't normally come into contact with, that little bit of additional help to get them through any tough time they might be facing.

Like with anything in life, the decision to write a book will come down to how much you really want to do it. And that is the question that I kick around a lot. Then I'll make a decision, as a result of which I'll actually get behind this book and do it – or not. Sounds simple. But of course, you're going to be asking yourself questions like, 'What's the point of it?' Well, on this occasion I had a clear answer to my doubts and questions.

I've spent around 20 years in the world of leadership and for such a long time, the story was always about the gold medallist – the winner! It was always about the person that had climbed the highest mountain. It was always about those people that have done incredible things and achieved brilliance. And yes, all of this is very inspiring, but there's always that bit at the back of your mind that says, 'But I'm not an Olympic athlete', or 'Well, I'm not going to be climbing that mountain, and actually I don't want to.'

I really felt that there was a need for people to have more conversations around what happens when life isn't going so well. When life gets difficult. When you're feeling like the walls are closing in or you are perhaps in the middle of your own storm. Bad things happen, it's normal, it's customary to us, it is relatable. Whether it's having a tough time in work, or the devastating news of cancer coming into your family, or whether you have lost your job, or been involved in a terrible accident. Whether it's that you just don't feel right. Whatever it is, it's when those negative times come, those difficult moments that I really think we need to have some more understanding. And hopefully, this is just what this book will do.

I looked at other people's difficult experiences, and to my own life, and considered what was both helpful and not in these types of situations. And soon, there was a real catalogue of ideas emerging about dealing with these tough times. And to go back to that question of how much you want to do something – this is what it came down to for me: can I do something that's going to help more people beyond social media and the coaching/development-type sessions that I already do? Something that was real and that was practical. Something broken down so simply and in one place that would mean that anyone could grasp it – wouldn't that be wonderful?

I'm never going to claim that I've had a tough life. In fact – even reflecting on my most difficult moments when compared to some people – it has probably been a charm. That being said, this book is about difficulties, so I have used my own life to examine how I dealt with those things, as well as looking at other people who have been through much, much worse. Personally, from right at the beginning of my learning journey there were obstacles. I didn't find school particularly easy. And it wasn't until I was 24 and in teacher training that I realised I had a learning difficulty. As a result of this, a lot of my adult life has been looking back and making connections between behaviour and experience and what I know now. Hindsight is a wonderful thing.

It was life changing. It was positive in many ways. I was careful to avoid the medical school syndrome of diagnosing myself of every possible disorder or learning difficulty just because I'd been to a fascinating seminar at university. There are some crazy things your brain can do. So, I tried very hard to stay open-minded about it all, but when I did the test, the results for dyslexia were very high, tipping into extreme. I was on the boundary of being an extreme dyslexic. At that point I thought, 'Well, that now makes sense, and I totally get it.' Nobody had put this label on me in school and so, like many others, I had missed out on the extra support. But I remember thinking that I had done all right without it. I had been to university, through teacher training, and had been coaching for coming up to almost a decade so I must have been doing something right. It was a realisation that I just had to work really hard, and while things might have taken me longer than they perhaps did for others, that was okay and in fact it was actually becoming a bit of a theme.

There are lots of things in my life where I've used what could be regarded as a potential negative to instead be a springboard to learn and to get better. And to face uncertainty and demonstrate resilience. I'm not talking life-threatening stuff that others have had to face, but regular everyday difficult stuff. I suppose my life is a testament to that, too. I've never been brilliant at anything. Genuinely, my skillset is tiny, absolutely tiny. But I know what I can do, and I know how to use those elements to better myself. The point is that I've got this passion and absolute unwavering belief that whatever the situation you're in, you can find stuff and leverage yourself and come through it and be better and move forward and life will go on. We'll find a path, we'll wrestle, as long as we're not scared of suffering – as my good mate Micky Mellon says, 'You've got to suffer, if you're not worried about suffering, we'll be all right.' And that's how this book has evolved.

There has been a lot of good stuff throughout my experiences. There have also been some challenges. I would say my departure from the school I was headteacher of was one of the hardest. My first book, *Educating Drew*, covered a lot of those wonderful experiences, but not so much of the ending. The ending was the hardest because it didn't just affect me. Yes, there was a 'me' element to it, but when something like that happens, you can see it is catastrophic. Harrop Fold in Little Hulton was my life – at the very least it was a major part of my life. I adored the area. I adored the school. I adored the staff. I was completely head over heels for the students. They were just amazing. And when somebody came along with what I perceived to be unfair accusations, it was an earth-shattering moment. It wasn't just a set of clouds that had landed. We were talking lightning, thunder, the full hit.

For me, the moment when it happened and the way in which it happened just didn't feel right – it didn't feel fair. It felt like I was a two-year-old stomping on the floor shouting, 'This isn't fair. It's not right.' But it wasn't so much that the issue was unfair; that was challenging enough. I knew I could get through that. We had made mistakes and mistakes can be overcome. It was definitely the following day, when the news of my suspension was leaked to the press and journalists were standing on the front lawn, and you see the impact of a life event on your loved ones and your significant others. That hurt. That is what was really hard to deal with. Of course, it was upsetting to me, but I guess I didn't even think of it at the time. The clouds, or storm, had arrived and I was only concerned about sheltering my family and loved ones from the downpour. It was that moment that was actually the most difficult. I'd had my tantrum, and then I was left watching with utter helplessness; it was now hurting those I care about.

In the quiet of my office, I asked myself over and over, 'How did this happen? How did I end up here?' There are lots of things you can look at. You can blame people. You can start to point fingers all over the place, but ultimately, I've ended up here and ultimately, I've had a role to play in it because I was the leader and as a leader you take responsibility.

Amongst all the chaos and upset and uncertainty I had a moment where it solidified what I already knew. I wasn't the best head teacher to have ever worked in a school, and was this the time to do something different? We've all got to provide money and help our family, but workwise, what is it that I loved? What was it that gave me work satisfaction? And, in that moment, I knew it boiled down simply to this: my passion is seeing people develop. Helping people to grow. Supporting people to flourish however is best for them; that is what I love.

As a leader in education, it was always about, 'How can we develop this whole area to have higher aspirations, to do what they want to do, to gain the life skills they need to take them beyond the world of school and into the real world?' Out of this whole horrible situation I realised something key in terms of myself and it was that out of this mess there could be something positive. And I now understood that I didn't want to just focus on developing people in schools – I wanted to work with as many people, in as many industries, as I could.

While I've had some wonderful success stories in my life and in my career, I don't think these really help distil who you are. I think it is in the moments of difficulty when you get this clarity, this real clear awareness – this is what I am, this is my makeup, this is what I stand for, these are my drivers. So again, in searching for the positives, tough times give us this.

In life, some things will really hurt. Some things will make you think – a lot. Some things are a complete car crash. Some things are just a scuff on the bumper. I think you've got to go through these things to bring you to where you are now. Having recently contracted COVID-19, this absolutely magnified that to me. I was really unwell. At one point I felt like I was unable to breathe, and I genuinely thought I might die. People in hospital were looking very concerned; therefore, I felt very concerned. I think that the whole experience added to that feeling of 'I'm really glad I'm still here'. And it was a huge reminder to really enjoy the journey, much more than you do now. Too often we run and rush into the next thing and then the next thing.

Sometimes we sit and stare at the past and go red with embarrassment. Or we sit still and don't move forward. I'm not saying be oblivious of the past or ride roughshod over those things. But it's a balance. Sometimes we can be guilty of trying to look too far forwards into the future. Who knows what that's going to actually look like? And looking too far back can also stop you from moving. If anything, COVID has taught us all that life can change at the flip of a coin, at any moment, so we need to accept what has brought us here and look to find ways forward. If we are lucky, we get 70 trips around the sun. That's it. That's 70 winters, 70 summers, and I'm 44 now. So, I could be way over halfway through my journey. And I now look at that kind of fragility of life and I think, 'Why do I care about that so much?' It might seem impossible on some days, some weeks and even for some months but whenever possible we need to try to enjoy the journey more. We're not going to be here forever.

I would also say leave people better than you found them as much as you possibly can. And finally, while life is not always going to be easy, it's not a bed of roses, we need to be ready for those tough times and not expect them to just happen to us. Enjoy the good times but be ready for those difficult times. And always remember, you can find a way through it.

During my difficult times, I looked to friends and family. It's as simple as that. I have my own things I do, breathing exercises, taking walks, reading, exercise. But when you are caught in a tough time or a struggle, I don't care how resilient you are, there will be times when your belief wavers. And in these times, it is absolutely, totally, perfectly 100% acceptable to borrow someone else's belief. I say it all the time, 'Life is a team sport. You need to have good people around you.' During my darkest moments I had friends and family there to offer support and I will never forget that. It's really important to use your support network. This is a leadership thing as well. Leaders say it's lonely at the top. Well, it's only lonely if you want it to be. I never led on my own, and I don't do life on my own. Because when I'm down, there'll be a good person there to pick me back up. When I'm struggling, there'll be a good person there to help me. And I want to make sure I'm there on the opposite side of that, to do exactly the same for others as was done for me. Network is crucial.

The whole reason for this book is having your own strategies. Someone might read this book and think, 'That won't work for me, but I do like that other idea, so I'll use that.' And that is great. If you take only one idea away and it helps you, then job done, because every idea and strategy won't fit or suit every person or situation. We need to find our own go-to mechanisms. What do we do in this scenario? Where do we go? We need our own personal plans and this plan would include having that network around you. That network is like the net that catches you when you are going through the motions of difficulty. Perhaps this book can be part of that safety net. In whatever way, I hope it helps you with any difficulties you may be facing.

Chapter 1

THE SCIENCE AND ART OF RESILIENCE

B ad stuff happens! The clouds will come. It's inevitable, it's relentless in some cases, and you can be absolutely sure it will happen to all of us. It doesn't matter what wonderful things we have, how lucky our situation, or simply just how stoic we are, the clouds will come. But before they do, let's go for a lovely picnic.

The Curious Picnic

Start simple. Close your eyes and imagine the perfect summer's day. You've decided to go for a picnic with your friends or family. It's a great day, you're all excited and about to start putting together everything you need for the perfect day out. So, what do you do? Well, first of all you delve into the fridge and you take a good look, and you can hardly believe your eyes when you find everything you need and you're thinking, 'Oh, wow. I didn't realise we had that, and that's my favourite food', and you start packing it up in the picnic basket you've been looking for an opportunity to use.

You grab a nice bottle of wine. And the kids' stuff is in there too – everything they like. The kids are behaving very well and when you say, 'Kids, go and get ready please' they do exactly as you ask. Everything is being done just as you wanted it, first time! It's a miracle! You've then loaded everyone into the car. You're off and you're driving to your favourite park. It's all going so well.

Now, you're thinking . . . 'It could be a bit busier today in the park because it's a beautiful summer's day.' But you arrive and there's a car parking space right outside the gate where you need to be, so with a smile on your face you then think 'This day could not get any better.'

You step out of the car, you get out your picnic basket and you're walking through the tree-lined pathways. People are out walking, children playing and laughing. There's that lovely smell of cut grass. The sky is blue, a few of the leaves have fallen on the ground. You've got your basket in your hand and it's swinging gently as you look around and then there it is – you find the ideal spot.

It's perfect. A bit of shade, but enough sunshine to enjoy. You spread your little tartan rug out on the ground, you put your hamper down, the kids are playing in the grass. It's a bit weird, they've not had a row, no one's stuck their finger in the other one's ear or anything like that. It's splendid.

You start pulling the food out and everything is still looking fresh, and nothing has got squashed or damaged in transit. But then, just as it was all going so well – disaster strikes! You reach for the bottle of wine (or non-alcoholic beverage of choice) and realise you've forgotten the corkscrew. You're raging. 'I don't believe it! Everything was going so well. I haven't brought the corkscrew!' And you really wanted that glass of crisp, cooled wine. You now have a problem. You've got to have this bottle of wine. And – open your eyes. You now have 15 seconds to think about how you would get into the bottle, 3-2-1, off you go.

When I discuss the above scenario with leaders and their teams, I would say about 80 per cent of people start sharing with me some elaborate, or not so elaborate, way of pushing the cork into the bottle, with string, with a finger. Some might even talk of chopping off the top of the champagne bottle with a sword or stabbing holes in the cork with a toothpick.

But what about using a shoe?

A few of you might know this, but one way to remove a cork without the key tool available is to simply remove any foil or seal on the bottle, then take off one of your shoes, put the bottle into the shoe and find a wall. With the bottom of the bottle firmly in the shoe – bash the shoe heel on the wall and slowly but surely the cork will begin to pop out. And you can do the rest. Voilà! Wine for your perfect picnic on a perfect day.

Now I realise that not having a corkscrew on your perfect picnic day out isn't exactly a tragedy – or anywhere close to the biggest problem we might face in our lives. In fact, if it is your biggest problem in life, you've probably got quite a few problems to deal with first, that you might've been overlooking. But, why on earth would I talk about having a picnic in relation to resilience?

Well, here is the key. Within this tiny frivolous example is a hidden gem about resilience that we don't often talk about. A tiny moment.

We can talk very easily about the fact that life has a way of knocking us to our knees. In life, sometimes, things just happen. The clouds come out of the blue, without warning, life smashes you in the face. A problem, an issue, personally or professionally things are going well and then something comes and just sideswipes you. 'Everyone has a plan until they get punched in the face', as the infamous Mike Tyson once said, and we can be sure that life is going to punch us in the face one day.

Now this is where I want to challenge other books about resilience and leadership. Like a bad cover version of the Chumbawumba song, so many intelligent folk will be telling you that when you get knocked down, you just need to get back up again. Up you get. Dust yourself off. Pull yourself up by your bootstraps. The Blitz Spirit. Go again. And again, and again. This is supposed to be resilience, but I don't think that it is. I would actually call this stupidity.

Running at a lamp post and getting knocked down only to get up again, and running again into the same lamp post and getting knocked down yet again sounds ridiculous. It is. If you read around the topic of resilience the vast majority of the experts will promote a quick response. A quick get-up-and-go response to getting knocked down, but I would like to challenge that as not actually being resilience.

It is a resilience of a sort. It's a toughness, but for me it's not the most interesting part of resilience. And it certainly doesn't help you to solve the problem or even help you move forward better than before.

For me, there is a moment before the 'bounceback-ability' happens, before you show the grit and desire to face that problem one more time. There is a moment before you show your strength and courage and your Chumbawumbaness – and that moment is all about curiosity.

When faced with a sealed bottle of wine at the picnic, what makes the curious few reach for the shoe and not a sharp implement? What makes someone want to push or pull the cork? A moment of curiosity.

And that's the hidden gem. In general, the shock, the anger, the frustration of being knocked down simply just stops the brain from thinking clearly. It stops your natural curiosity from asking 'why?' and 'what?' about the situation – massively important questions you need to ask about the moment and your response to those clouds arriving. Consequently, if you're not thinking curiously, there is a huge probability that you're just going to get knocked down with the exact same problems again and again.

What does Starbucks sell?

So, here's another question – what does Starbucks sell? Coffee, right? It seems like a logical answer to even the most snobbish of coffee aficionados – Starbucks sell coffee. Well, they did. Right up until

2008 that is, when Harold Schultz went back to Starbucks and found a coffee-selling company facing near financial ruin. What he then did was this: rather than trying to just tinker around the edges, when they were close to financial ruin, he actually got curious about the company and said, 'What is Starbucks? Are we going to be the best coffee maker?' It's not controversial to say that their focus wasn't on providing the greatest tasting coffee, like your local artisan store. They could have tried to go into this high-quality coffee market, but Schultz acknowledged that other people were doing it better.

So, what do you do when you're getting beaten down by competitors and you are facing those dark clouds? Well, amongst other things, he brought all the managers from all the stores around the world to New Orleans in the USA in 2009. The whole endeavour cost the company a reported $33 million. You can imagine the conversation at the boardroom meeting. Howard Schultz walks in for the second time as CEO to deal with the company's financial issues and he says, 'Right everyone – I'm going to spend 33 million dollars retraining all the managers of all our stores. This is going to be the kickstart we need.'

But what was his question, what was his curious thought and why would he think this could change coffee selling for the next ten years? He realised one thing from the knock-down and beating they were taking as a company – 'We're not in the coffee market, we're in the coffee experience market.'

And that is how Schultz and Starbucks created and propagated something called 'the third space'. A space so familiar to us all that we forgot it existed until a pandemic and lockdown came along. You have work, you have home, and you've got that space in between – Starbucks. The coffee shop that bridges the two, waiting for the train, meeting a friend, needing a change of scenery, you all have your own version of why you go into Starbucks – for the free Wi-Fi, to read the paper or a book, to meet your friends, to buy some food, and then a drink. Lots of people go to Starbucks and don't even want to buy the coffee. The result went down in business and cultural history. Schultz got curious when the company was at its lowest point. They didn't just bounce back, they bounced back smarter.

A similar story happened with Steve Jobs at Apple. In 1997, he came back to Apple and, in 1998, he was appointed CEO. As was the case with Schultz, this was a return to a company he had worked at before. And as with Starbucks, there were issues. He was rejoining Apple in a very crowded technology market, at a time when they were not winning. What most people would have done at Apple, as our friends at Chumbawumba tell us, is to have got back up and pushed hard and fast with an attempt to compete with Dell and Microsoft in the crowded personal computer market. However, Jobs got curious when Apple were at the bottom. They were close to ruin, and I imagine him saying to his team something like, 'What is this brand? We're about innovation, we're about sexy products. We're about design and exclusivity and something different. We're not just another grey box in a cubicle.'

Following what I think would have been long and probably difficult discussions with the team and board members and against all advice, Apple came out with the iPod. You can almost envisage the conversations that took place. 'Steve, you're having a laugh. It won't work my man because Dell have tried the MP3 player down the road in Silicon Valley and it didn't work there so it's not going to work for us either.' But he had looked harder at this problem and retorted with the understanding of why people didn't want to have an MP3 player. And for Jobs, the answer was that people could no longer be bothered with getting CDs, downloading them onto a computer and then putting them on the iPod. People did still do this, but he didn't think that was true of the less technologically proficient mass market that he was aiming at. Jobs' response was clear and calm and will have no doubt gone something like, 'Don't worry about that, I've thought about that. We're going to create a platform called iTunes. An on-demand music service that you can use to load your music on to the iPod with the click of the button', and with that he changed the whole computer market and made downloading music mainstream. All this success was a direct result of him getting curious. When they were down at the bottom, like Schultz, he got curious and found a way to do something differently.

He then repeated this with the iPhone and iPad. Both of which were products that had been thought of and launched in different formats and previously failed. But Jobs kept being curious, looking at the alternatives, the reasons why previous portable phones or laptop hybrids hadn't quite made it to market. The result is a generation-defining piece of technology that sits in our pocket against the views of successful market leaders who had argued 'people don't need data on a phone', and that 'no one wants apps or functionality on a tablet when you have a laptop'. Those companies dealt with the threat by doing more of the same. Apple, however, took the beating and got curious.

When the clouds come it's not enough to be resilient and tough, we must ignite this curious practice. If you can get curious, you can find the energy and the positivity you need to come back smarter. When you really understand what knocked you down and really start to look at the big picture, you can get perspective. Curiosity, I truly believe, helps you to zoom out, rather than just being zoomed in and this perspective is what starts to give people a bit of energy.

Beyond the Theory

So how do you do it? The theory is great – you're down on the ground looking up at the clouds, but what do you actually *do* to get curious? Because when you're down there you aren't alone in thinking how hard it is, just to stay even vaguely upright.

The first thing is, I think you've got to learn as much as you can about what's just happened. As Jim Collins says in his books *Good to Great* and *Built to Last,* 'you've got to confront the brutal facts'. You've just got to confront the brutal facts and go head-on into it and get really curious. You can't ignore it; you can't hide away from it. You must just front up to it and look at it. That's a real energy giver. Not filtering with a sense of pity and emotional crisis – simply looking at what happened. Just to let you know at this point, you will have to feel all the emotions relating to it, but for now that's probably not going to help you move further forward. Matthew Syed talks about 'black box thinking' for these kinds of situations. When an airplane crashes we revisit the crash site, open the black box and read the recorded information that led up to the disaster. That's how to learn from the failure. What has gone on here? Trying to learn as much as possible, as it is that learning that is going to be crucial.

In all honesty this isn't an easy process. Looking at a disaster that you will undoubtedly feel emotionally connected to is not a simple thing. It takes humility. For the majority of people, they won't want to look. They won't want to learn because when the clouds come, their instinct is to hide away from the facts or fail to acknowledge any involvement. Pride or fear. Fight or flight. They're instincts, but they don't necessarily involve curiosity. And they can't help you from repeating the same issue time and time again. However often you hide from the rain clouds, it doesn't stop the rain. Humility isn't about feeling sorry for yourself. It does require you to acknowledge that sometimes your natural ability and talent will help you to succeed, but sometimes that just isn't enough. The first element to consider when you're knocked to your knees and embarking on the curiosity ride, or when those clouds come, is that you have got to learn. Learn about what happened, and I think you have got to drive that through humility.

The second part to this curious process is unlearning. That might sound curious in itself but what

I mean by this is asking yourself, 'What do I normally do in these situations and is that helpful right now?' I've been asked the question myself, 'Well, what would you do differently?' When leaders reply to this question with 'Nothing, nothing, because even the things that weren't quite right were a learning experience', I might respond with, 'Yeah, okay. Nice one for being clever', because actually I am sure everybody, in every situation, could do something, if not everything, differently. We could have written this chapter differently; we could have found different examples or changed the order or used different vocabulary. There is always something you can look back at and think you could have done better. It takes humility to accept that and curiosity to consider what that might be. It doesn't mean this is a right or wrong situation. It's a 'let's learn from what happened' situation. Curiosity leading to progress.

Part of that is a general acceptance that 'unlearning' is key. Even if you nail something, it's important to remember the fact that what will work now, or what got you to where you are now, won't always keep you there. And it definitely won't get you to your next level because the new level will be different and therefore requires different detail and input and output. So, in life, we're constantly unlearning what we have done before. There are certain things I do and have done in the past that

I have had to unlearn. I have to strip it out and say to myself, 'Drew, that is a pothole, that is a pitfall, that is something that's going to trip you up.' And actually taking those things out and snagging them and saying, 'Right, that won't work now. Even if it has in the past, that will not work anymore', gives us the opportunity of understanding our situation and it's making sure that we remove those things that are going to trip us up. And if it feels like I'm talking to myself a lot, it's because I am. Your strength and positivity come from you – but we'll talk about that later.

The final element is to relearn. People talk about fail forward, fail better, fail faster, make mistakes matter, keep learning new ways of doing things. I do think we almost relearn how we handle those situations. And it can be quite daunting because we quite like our fixed habits: 'So, if this happens, this is what I do.' But seldom do those things work time and time again. Particularly in a leadership context, never mind in a life context. That might have worked pre-COVID, or it might have worked pre-Brexit, or pre-Trump, but it won't work anymore.

Looking at sport for example – what Manchester City did a few seasons ago didn't then work in the season when Liverpool dominated the whole league and eventually won. And actually, what Liverpool did in their winning year has not been the same as they are doing now or will do in the years to come. They will have to unlearn some stuff and relearn new and better ways of doing things. Olympic athletes who win gold medals in multiple games don't keep doing the same thing over and over again. Wimbledon champions change coaches and trainers because they're looking for the next improvement or variation. The tiny, but continual improvement, the marginal gains stuff. And of course, if I still haven't convinced you on this, remember Einstein's definition of insanity, 'doing the same things over and over again and expecting different results'. In short, change nothing – nothing changes.

And this is maybe where to see this moment, the chance to unlearn, the chance to be curious, the chance to try and take something informative and positive from the situation. Because after all, we never know what is around the corner. I won't know what's around the corner for me and I certainly don't know what's around the corner for anybody else. But what I do know is that at some point we're likely to be sideswiped, knocked to our knees and the clouds are going to come. It's going to happen to us personally, it's going to happen to us professionally. The sticky stuff is going to hit the fan at some point in our lives.

Getting Up Smarter

I think if we can be curious when those bad times come, this is the hidden gem. Most advice about pulling yourself up, dusting yourself off, getting back in the race – is skewed. It doesn't just get us back to our feet, because, well, it is not just about getting back to your feet. Neither is it about getting back to your feet as quickly as you can. Getting back up quickly can lead you to being knocked down harder, or even worse – knocked down permanently. Running towards the problem requires some thought. Not just speed and aggression. We have to be smarter as a result of what's happened. And unless you're curious, you can't drag that learning through to making that resilience become an actual muscle and a thing that we can use.

People talk about resilience being a muscle and they talk about how you've got to train your resilience. But if you just get knocked down and get back up again you will weaken the muscle. The muscle won't get stronger. Emotionally or psychologically, we actually get used to the negative not the positive. We have to develop the muscle, not overload it. We must progress the muscle and we have to be specific about how we train it. The muscle has to get better, and it has to be continually flexed and I think it's done by curiosity, which is done by learning, unlearning, and relearning.

In all honesty, this talk of muscles and resilience still sounds like we're talking in big theoretical ideas. It makes sense if you're a CEO sitting around brainstorming and blue-sky thinking. Those three parts of curiosity will make absolute sense – learning, unlearning, and relearning – and might even be part of your own staff training. But what is the practical application of these ideas in everyday life? What does it look like?

It looks like the moment you are knocked down and you look up and take a pause. Imagine that. The freeze-frame. The moment stops – like in the movies – and you can see it all. You. The thing that knocked you down. And this pause is the moment to get up smarter and better than before. Anyone in the world can get back up from a knock-down but why wouldn't you want to get up smarter and better?

In *Man's Search for Meaning,* Viktor Frankl wrote about the big difference between reacting and responding. He famously survived the prisoner-of-war camps in the 1940s, so his viewpoint on resilience and his understanding of how to get up from tragedy in an intelligent and healthy way is more valid than most.

Going back to our picnic – a reaction is you realising you have no corkscrew to open your wine, feeling angry, packing up, and storming off home. Or alternatively, you just put away the wine and go without. Both are reactions to the situation – fight, flight, or hide from the problem. But you're losing something. You either lose the picnic or lose an enjoyable part of it. Is there a way to gain something from an otherwise less than desirable situation?

What we need is a space to respond and Frankl talks about needing a gap between stimulus and response. Trying to extend that reaction time – from knee-jerk, to something longer and giving yourself a moment – a gap. He says that in life, if you just take that gap your response will be smarter and better.

When we don't have a gap between the stimulus and response, we can end up doing some very stupid things, even if we have good instincts. A gap is needed. A moment to pause and respond instead of getting back up and running towards the fist that just knocked us down. Now what do you do in that pause? What will be the foundation of your response? You're knocked down. You look up. You take a moment to consider your response. And what?

In her book *Option B*, Sheryl Sandberg talks powerfully about the unexpected death of her husband and the huge impact this had. Grief is arguably one of the biggest knock-downs we can suffer. Anything else might be big but there is still something to confront and something to realise – when death confronts us, personally, we are gone. We are no more. Anything less than death is probably something you can overcome. But this doesn't help us in the moment and when faced with grief we might believe we will never overcome it.

I would say I've read quite a lot about grief because while I'm interested in the process of how you move anyone to acceptance at any time in their lives, I think there is an added layer to overcome in grief when moving to that stage of acceptance. And what's interesting about this process is that there are two ways you can approach it. You can approach it in a reactive way, like I'm just going to go through the stages of denial, anger, and bargaining as in the Kubler-Ross grief cycle. The 'what if' questions – what if I hadn't left at the time I did, what if I hadn't gone out in the car, what if we hadn't chosen that park, what if I'd have chosen a different job, what if, what if and so on. And then you may go to depression, then you move to acceptance. But what a lot of people in grief counselling are now saying, like Dr Lucy Hone, is that we need to be proactive (the second way), and we actually need to push people to move through these stages. Let's not sit and wait for it to happen, let's work on it and explore it and hit it head on. Your curiosity allows you to confront the brutal facts and before leaping back up and running into a brick wall, you can think and consider and work out your response. We still need to go forward and move towards our problem – that's unavoidable. But you've got to create the gap, and then you've got to go back towards the problem, with some form of way to attack it – something that's called post-traumatic growth.

Post-Traumatic Growth (PTG)

I am assuming most people have heard of post-traumatic stress disorder: the reoccurrence of feelings and emotions and physical reactions to a trauma, after the fact. It's a commonplace phrase that has oftentimes now been diluted to the point of not really explaining or helping those who suffer from it. But what about post-traumatic growth (PTG)?

Post-traumatic growth is the key to how we get back up, and from Sheryl Sandberg's inspiring book it provides a reason for getting up. PTG suggests that if we handle grief or trauma in the right way, it can actually be a time of growth. For me, I think that it's the reason to get up, the reason to pause and consider a response, the reason to be curious. PTG may encourage people to be curious.

The reason I think people don't get curious at the moment they're knocked down is because of a lack of something Quoidbach et al. (2014) labelled as 'emodiversity' or 'The variety and relative abundance of the emotions that humans experience'. We don't attempt to work out what we're feeling, we just feel. We just label it broadly as good or bad, box it, and get back up and run towards the lamp post. We don't really work on understanding our full array of emotions. We simply accept an emotion – 'Oh well, I feel good', 'I feel bad', 'I feel happy', or 'I feel sad'. We don't actually consider the emodiversity that is at interplay with one another.

I believe the growth in PTG can come from going towards the trauma, being curious about it, labelling it and understanding it and coming to terms with it. You then can grow to higher levels of, for example, happiness, than you had before the trauma. That's the positive. That's the learning part. And it is how the curiosity that is natural to you can make the trauma seem smaller and more manageable and easier to overcome.

We've all been in the situation when something has gone bad. I remember a particularly dark time in my life when everything had been turned upside down after leaving my job and I felt numb. I'd been knocked down and I couldn't really feel anything. I remember thinking, 'How do I feel right now?' and it was a bit numb, really. I couldn't feel anything for myself. Nothing. Didn't feel sad, happy, angry. I felt I'd let my family down. My mum was crying on the phone. But actually, myself, I just felt numb. But when I actually started to think, 'Right, what is really going on here?' I created the gap – the gap between the stimulus and response. 'Okay, how do I feel? I feel let down. I feel aggrieved but actually I'm also feeling that this is deeply unfair and unjust, this is not right.'

So, then I started to focus on that thing and I went right into my emotions and got curious about that. 'How am I really feeling in this moment?' And I wasn't upset, I wasn't angry. I was like – 'This is unjust, this is wrong.' The best way to describe it, and this is an experience we've probably all had when the clouds come, you feel a bit like a two-year-old who's stamping their feet shouting, 'It's not fair! It's not fair! It's not fair!' and I know it's childish, but it's how I felt at the time.

So, is it really that bad to feel like that? It's complex. You can give into it and blame the world for your pain and suffering. You can feel ashamed for being so childish. You can feel angry and sad for the things broken or lost. The range of emotions is diverse. The more you acknowledge the emodiversity and give in to your curiosity, you find yourself walking towards the trauma and it can start to make sense. And like the peeking behind the curtain in the *Wizard of Oz*, the problem doesn't seem so big or so vast when you realise it's lots of different emotions all stacked together.

In this particular case I ended up on the phone to family talking through the details and the more we looked at it and the more we acknowledged the emotions and allowed ourselves to be curious, the more the situation seemed bearable and almost verging on the ridiculous. At that moment, I even managed to laugh. It might have looked like I was hysterical, but I was laughing at the events that had brought me to this point, at myself, at my reaction. And it might seem like I've trivialised it and I certainly would never want to do that. But sometimes it's good to look at it head on and say, just as my older brother Ross has always said, 'You are still alive – and that's all that matters.' And regain some perspective. In life, what really matters? If it's a death, it's a cataclysmic, chaotic, awful, shocking, can't-get-your-head-around-it moment. But there are not many things in life that happen like that, thankfully. Actually, the rest of it, if we go towards it, whilst painful I think it can be helpful. Particularly in a work context, we can go towards it. We find growth by being curious and looking very hard at the problem, while accepting all those emotions surrounding it.

Reframing

Don't get me wrong, this doesn't happen immediately. We've got to confront it and create the gap, but then actually seeing it as a chance to learn and grow is difficult. In the immediate aftermath it's hard to separate the emotions and think rationally. So, while I would never have said this over the first weekend or on the Friday when it all started kicking up, by the Sunday I had started to think, 'Right, I need to reframe this in my head, this is going to be a different part of my life.' And then, 'Do you know what? I'm going to learn a lot about these scenarios', and because I'm a leadership geek and I'm always looking at things that I think I could put together that would help a leader and others, straightaway I'm starting to learn about this scenario of a complete car crash in your life career-wise, and actually what that could mean.

I suppose the best way of talking about this is to reframe it, like Martin Seligman when he talks about disputation in his book *Learned Optimism*. So, the adversity comes and Seligman proposes an A-B-C-D model. The A is for the adversity. The B is what do we believe, what do we start thinking at that time, and because of negativity bias, we're more likely to see the negative and protect ourselves and protect the ones we love, that starts catastrophising – the C. The consequence of this is that we feel and know that we're in a right mess. But Seligman says that A-B-C happens all the time. Where he suggests we move next is towards the D – disputation. This is the really important bit. The D is about disputing the beliefs. You're through the A-B- and C, now it's time to pause and start asking questions. Knowing this was vital. I really did start to think, 'Do you know what, my wife's upset, but she's healthy. Overall, she's healthy. We've got a house and a roof over our head. I've got my health. I can put food on the table.' It was about reframing the situation and it wasn't me polishing a turd or rolling a turd in glitter. It was actually thinking, everyone has their own problems and obstacles to face and while this is absolutely terrible, there's a lot of people in this world worse off than me and I have loads of things to be grateful for. Disputing what has happened to you allows you to reframe the whole event. It allows you to gain some time to see perspective. It's not easy, but that's because we're emotional beings.

Of course, it's much easier to give this advice to someone else than it is take it yourself. And that's the hardest thing to do with reframing. If you just sit there for a minute, realise what you're doing, why you're there, what you're there for and you talk about that, that's hard. It's much easier if someone's standing looking over at you and says, 'Well you need to do this.' It's a bit like watching a boxing match or watching someone play football. It's always easier to comment on what's gone wrong. Being in the moment itself, however, is very hard. Can you give yourself the right advice? Sometimes it feels like it is too hard to do. It's too hard to see the reality of the situation or give yourself that moment or that advice. That's why reframing often needs other people. Not always, but sometimes. The other people around you can really help you to gain perspective, and that allows you to dispute what has happened.

For me – I didn't do it on my own. I am extremely fortunate to have some great people around me, and all of them were helping me. I had what I call my A-team around me who came in and reminded me 'Look, this isn't the end of the world. This can be the start of something. You can get through this', and they were helping me to reframe. But even if they aren't there all of the time, and you do end up alone at times, you can still work through it. You can still reframe the moment. I just think that having a team around you to support you can speed up the process. Everything is easier from an outside perspective.

It's not so simple to achieve this when you're in the middle of a situation. People who gain perspective the fastest will sometimes get back up quicker. However, for a lot of us, we struggle with this. Our heads are down and if we manage to get up, we just keep on piling through and nothing happens, or we hit the same thing again. It's hard to accomplish. But not impossible. To continue with the boxing analogy: when you've been knocked on your backside and the fight's over, who's the first one in? You're still dazed and reeling. Not sure quite what happened or what went wrong. Struggling to focus. But your team is there. Your corner has come out to remove your gumshield, wipe your brow, little gestures to show support. Sometimes they'll physically lift you to your feet, sometimes it will just be that word of encouragement. But you do get up. Everyone gets up finally. You may have lost the round, but you will get up. You may have lost the match, but you will get up.

So, who's your team? This is an important part of how you get up and face the problem with curiosity. Who's the team around you? Who is that A-team? They are going to be able to support you to find the way forward. This is the hard part for many who find themselves alone, or unable to reach out, or just with only themselves as a resource. However, if it's you alone, a family and group of friends around you, a work colleague, or a listening voice on the end of a phone support line – there can be a team to help you with providing that disputation. As I always say, 'Life is a team sport.'

Optimism From the Floor

So, you've got your team around you. You're starting to reframe what has happened. You're feeling curious about what led to the knock-down. What next? For many leaders, it is that version of the Chumbawumba lyric 'We get knocked down, we get up again!' but we really shouldn't be so naïve. The issue is not so simple, and the solution definitely needs to be much more deliberate. A cheery 'Smile, it can't be that bad!' might help some, but it's not real support. It's just a plaster over a massive wound. In leadership terms, the advice you need is about some 'realistic optimism'.

Like Winston Churchill's 'brutal optimism', this is going to be hard and difficult, but we can still get through it. You've heard it before. It's not new information, but when you pause and reframe, to acknowledge the difficulty of the situation, it can become easier to look at it with optimism. The longer you look at those clouds and remember that you've seen them before, and you've experienced rain, wind, and storms, and that the sun will come out again. It's clichéd, but after every winter, there's a springtime ahead.

In the book *Stronger* by Dennis K McCormack, Douglas A Strouse, and George S Everly Jnr, they talk about 'active optimism' – believing that you can get through difficulty. And I think there's a major part of having to be realistic in your optimism. Controlled and thoughtful in your approach to the positive. You can't have the rose-tinted specs coming out, you've got to be realistic but you need to be optimistic, 'I am going to get through this.' And I remember I kept saying to myself, 'This too shall pass.' It will pass. This is going to pass, it's not forever. The permanence thing. It doesn't have to be forever. Even with grief. And that's life.

Unlikely compatriots, Rocky Balboa and Laura McInerney CEO of Teacher Tapp, both share the same thought process in relation to this: 'Life isn't all sunshine and rainbows'. In a conversation Laura once commented, 'You've got to imagine that if you were in a boxing match people will want to see you get a bloody nose. They don't want to see you in a boxing match, no matter how good you are and no one put a glove on you. They want to see you take a hit and life is full of hits.' So realising this fact is important. Even if you don't want the paranoia of thinking people are willing you to fail. Knowing this helps you to pause. It helps you to reframe. It helps you to gain some sense of optimism about what's next. If that is the least you do in that moment whilst you're on the floor, feeling bruised and battered, then it's a good place to start. When Laura said this, it was a big moment for me because I thought, 'She's right. People often don't want to see you glide through life untouched. Whether it's me or anybody else gliding without a problem, or a drama because that's just unrealistic and a bit galling. That stuff only happens in the fairy tales.'

The world is a whole lot more cynical. So that even in modern fairy tales, it doesn't really happen there either. Even your Disney heroes are a little bit rough around the edges and have to fight through stuff to get to the end. The social narrative has changed. No one has an easy ride, no one's perfect, because no one wants to see that – it just makes people feel worse about themselves. If someone's perfect and does things perfectly, it can make us reflect negatively on ourselves and we don't like that. Whereas, if we see someone flawed and broken and a little bit bashed around, who has had to overcome things, then we like that, we sympathise and empathise. Not necessarily the full-on underdog, but we like to see our own issues and problems and difficulties reflected in what we watch and read and view. Perfection doesn't help us when the clouds come. Delusion doesn't help us either. Realistic optimism based on a moment of clear thinking. That's what can help us to get back up.

What's really key, though, for leaders to understand is you're not going to do this in just one sitting and leaders are impatient, they want to get it done now.

You've got to start the process, but you need to come back the next day, or at a later time or date. And it took me a while to get my head around that. I look at the example of Tiger Woods. He was a hero for everyone, 'Do it like Tiger.' Big Nike adverts. Huge sponsorship. Massive following. Champion golfer. Title after title. He was the man! Then his life went kaboom with allegations of sex addiction, drug addiction, drug and drink driving offences, a car crash of a life, and then a professional injury. He went from top dog to bottom dog so fast.

In 2013, amongst popular opinion polls he was ranked the third or fourth most hated athlete on the planet. Fast forward just a few years, in 2019 he wins the Master's again and he went from this bottom dog figure to top dog again. Or underdog to top dog. And I think there are so many examples of where people like to see the phoenix rising from the ashes. Six years where he went away. Six years to reframe. Retrain. Physically, mentally, psychologically. He had to unlearn the world that loved and worshipped him. He had to unlearn everything that was positive about his life previously, because when he came back, no one was looking at him in the same way. Think for a moment what that takes to bounce back from such a moment. All his clouds came at once and he still came back. So, what stops us all coming back just like Tiger?

The godfather of positive psychology, Martin Seligman, has written a lot about this. He says that there are three key things that hinder resilience and recovery.

The first thing is personalisation, which of course is easy to do. It's where you think it's all your fault. You start to believe everything's down to you, 'I'm cursed. This is all on me! It's all my fault! No one's ever had this happen to them before.'

The second element is pervasiveness, where we think the problem or issue is going to spread into all aspects of our lives. Personally, I spent many hours thinking this way: 'I'm a complete failure at everything because this one thing has happened to me. I can't do anything, I'm a terrible dad, I'm a bad husband, I'm a useless brother, I'm a rubbish son, I'm a dreadful friend. I'm no good at leadership. I don't understand education. . .' This one bad thing is pervasive and now encompasses everything.

And the final aspect that Seligman talks about is permanence. The more you think those things in that context, the more permanent it will become. If we don't pause and unlearn that train of thought that is personal and pervasive, the more permanent it will become.

That's why we need to reframe and gain perspective. Given the right context, all problems can seem less damaging, less personal, less pervasive. With our A-team in support, or simply that moment to pause before responding we can contextualise our problems. Some people write this down – journalling has been a lifeline for me. But whether you write it down or think it to yourself or talk it through with others, it's time to dispute the situation and ask some serious questions.

I think in any moment of difficulty we have probably all done Martin Selligman's three things: I certainly did personalise, I did make it pervasive, and I did think it was permanent – I thought I'd never work again. At the time of my suspension, we had only just invested money in building a home office in the garden using our savings and I remember thinking, 'What on earth do we do now?' I couldn't see the positive at all. I couldn't reframe it. But six months down the line, the fact of the matter is that a home office has been a total godsend for me and our business, which we now run from home. But at the time, I couldn't see it. Reading back over the Sheryl Sandberg book, I realised that very often in life you can't have option A. You can't always have the solution you want. So, it's not just about the fact you've been knocked down. You need to look at what you do when you get up, and sometimes it's just not possible to continue from where you left off. Option B is the reframed alternative, the perspective you didn't have, and the chance to be positive moving forwards – the silver lining in those clouds.

Knowing this and choosing this are two very different things. In this situation, I hate to say it – but you do have to choose your attitude. Another hard task, but it is something you can build in as a daily habit. Like when you're picking your shirt out of the wardrobe in the morning, you pick your attitude. It sounds a little cheesy, but I've learned to now be one of those people that say, 'Well, I can choose what I want to be today.' I know I felt awful and I felt the lowest ever and it was starting to become pervasive. I thought I was no good to anyone or anything at times. Because, when it really gets you, I suppose it really gets you. And I did personalise it. I took it all on my own shoulders, I thought it affected the whole of life. But you have to dispute this. You have to find that perspective, and you have to choose a positive attitude to move forward with option B.

How to Find Option B

It still comes down to the 'how'. How do you ensure you have people around you that you can talk to about this? How do you find the physical and emotional strength to take the breath and ask yourself the right questions?

You can't have option A, so you have to start getting curious about what option B is. And it's a process. From recognising your emodiversity, trying to reframe the situation, getting your A-team around you, finding gaps to be able to be curious. Personally, I think reading about people who've had difficult times, and journalling these things helps, but that's not for everyone. I think there are a number of things that you can always learn and so many good strategies that I believe will really help us to be resilient. For some reason, I like to see it written down on paper, and I'm not writing a novel here, but because I know no one's going to see it, it keeps my thoughts in order. I write in pencil so that I can make loads of mistakes. And I actually write what's happened. I don't really write how I'm feeling, but that's supposed to be very powerful too, and there's a lot of research on that.

I write what's happened. And when I see it on paper, it helps me to recognise what it really is, rather than doing that catastrophising. I think the important thing is once you've done something once, you can do it again.

It seems like a lot of this process has to be about that thing that other people are always better at – giving advice. Everybody's better at giving advice to someone else in someone else's situation, but when it comes to the arrival of the clouds, you have to actually be able to do that to yourself too. You can use your friends and your A-team around you to help you see that, but at some point along the line, you yourself have to confront and then dispute the problem.

Putting words that are yours onto a page is a great way to do this, and then those words are not yours anymore. They are now a list of facts that you can reframe and give advice to. They are someone's problem, and you're going to help them to solve it. Even by the process of writing it down, you're making it 'other', and that I think is helpful. It's similar to going for a walk and moving from a different space, and how it can make you feel different just walking rather than sitting. The otherness allows you to maybe see *you* differently.

This is part of the reframing moment – the moment before the response – and it's about balancing that relationship between emotion and logic. It's what we experience when we get knocked down, or the rain comes – the emotion overwhelms us because it's horrible. When the clouds come, the emotion does grab you. But actually, when you look at the logical stuff, you often find that most of the emotion isn't based upon anything real or tangible or useful. You look up at what's knocked you down and realise – that's all this is. It's not about moving away from the emotions, because you've got to know how you feel, but you've got to add logic in there as well. And I think that's the difference between a reaction and a response. Your response is considered, reframed, based on advice, a reaction based on emotion. Resilience is many things, but a huge part of it is giving yourself space to do exactly this. The science of resilience unfolds through the art of creating space to consider, reframe, and respond to getting knocked down.

Chapter 2

TO DO
COURAGE

Courage is the most important of all virtues, because without courage you can't practice any other virtue consistently.

—Maya Angelou

For me, courage is the catalyst for most things. It's a spark and a driving force. It's what makes things happen. It's a doer, a maker, a mover, and a shaker. I believe it's what we must use to get us through what is trying to knock us back.

In the previous chapter, we talked about how resilience needs to be re-examined to ensure we make the smartest choices when the clouds come. And the same applies to courage. The more I looked at the word 'courage', the more it needed unpicking. What is it? What does it enable you to do? And how do you find it when things go wrong?

I have written about and talked to lots of people about courage over the past ten years and if you ask anyone whether they think courage is important, most will answer 'yes' pretty quickly. In any context of life, whether in leadership of a company, of a school, of a sports team, of your own life, courage is important. There will be times in your life when the clouds come and you're going to have to be courageous.

Perhaps, too, there have been times in your life when it was going really well, and you also needed to be courageous. If we are safe in our comfort zones, it is courage that helps us embrace the new or find the next challenge. Courage helps us move forward and can be the catalyst in times that are both positive and negative.

Simply put, courage is the magic that allows you to go outside of your comfort zone into that stretch zone and start to learn and grow. As Angelou says, courage is fundamental to probably every other virtue. Because without courage, what else have you got? Change doesn't happen. You aren't able to be resilient when the clouds come. Without courage, in small and big ways, you don't move. You simply don't do anything.

I take an interest in all forms of human endeavour, and I'm very interested at seeing this in businesses, whether they're doing well, whether they're just ticking over, or whether they're really struggling. But particularly when businesses or industries are struggling, what is it that people do?

Be More Apple, or Be More Hedgehog?

We talked about Apple before and how the curiosity of Steve Jobs propelled Apple forward and this fits nicely within this framework of courage too.

Jobs returned to the company in 1997 with the title of interim CEO, and the business at this time was one of many fighting for a slice of the personal computer market. They were in real trouble. Microsoft was dominant in the computer world and part of the magic of Jobs as a leader and businessman was the courage he possessed to go against all the 'experts' within and outside of his company to launch the iPod.

This doesn't mean that every 'maverick' idea is going to work – look at some of the colossal failures of other business greats such as Richard Branson and Elon Musk. But the common theme they share with Jobs is this concept of courage 'to do'. When everyone told Jobs that the iPod wouldn't work, that people have tried the MP3 player, and it just doesn't have that mass market appeal, he stuck to his guns. He was curious about what was stopping the MP3 player from succeeding, and he had the courage to try something different.

In this particular situation, he had noticed that people didn't want to download and then transfer all of their CDs onto a computer to upload them again to another device. Exhausting, techy, and time consuming. So, he made it easier for the everyday music listener – and he created iTunes. All music, all available and easy to download onto your portable iPod. His curiosity and courage were catalysts for a revolution in how we listen to music. We can still buy the physical form, the vinyl, the CDs, etc., but look at what the digital music file has done for how we access music – on our phones, laptops, TVs – everything is streamed and accessible away from the physical form of music that it always had been until this point. Courage and curiosity working together to change something. It's a wonderful example of how courage compels action. Just imagine how the world might have been different if the iPod was just another MP3 player, or a Discman.

It's definitely a challenge for anyone struggling to find possibilities or have the courage to keep on moving during tough times. Running a failing business that was previously successful must be so difficult. The temptation to return to what you did before, or simply to keep doing what you do now and hope for the best, is often prevalent amongst companies in these very circumstances.

In 2004, LEGO were in that exact situation. Numbers were collapsing, and they were in a right mess. In the eighties and nineties, LEGO was the go-to toy. A consistent performer that would have been found in most homes with children – including my own. Everyone had LEGO. But the rise of cheap and accessible electronic toys meant that they were being surpassed and overtaken by their competitors. They just couldn't regain their position in the toy market. Now, it is true that they could have tried to revolutionise their product – go electric. They could have tried a bold innovation like Apple. But instead, they took courage in a whole different direction. They hunkered down and carried out what Jim Collins in his book *Good to Great* refers to as the Hedgehog concept.

In the battle between a hedgehog and a fox, the fox is superior to the hedgehog in pretty much every area. They are a predator with teeth and claws and an agility that enables them to hunt and scavenge effectively. But the hedgehog has one advantage over the fox – it can curl up into a tight little ball, with its spikes pointing outwards, and protect every part of its vulnerable body. It doesn't stop the hedgehog from being tossed around, but it stops the fox from getting its teeth around it. Hedgehog – 1, Fox – nil.

In this nature/business scenario, LEGO showed courage to go fully hedgehog and focus on what it did best: they made the brick. LEGO knew they were the company that produces a wondrous brick that allows people to experiment, get creative, and build. They courageously chose to focus on what they knew and what was at the heart of their brand and at the core of their business. And the rest, as they say, is history. The global financial crash came, low-cost toys were popular again and LEGO returned as a top seller. The hedgehog took a bold but different decision, and the company is still thriving today.

Both Apple and LEGO have continued to show courage, to innovate, to stick to their principles, and they are still leading in their markets. In contrast, however, are those brands and companies that have crashed and burned. They failed to show courage at key moments. One example of this is Blockbuster. For those of a certain generation, the Friday night trip to get videos and snacks from their local video rental shop was a weekly staple. But as technology and consumer habits changed, Blockbuster had the opportunity to buy Netflix (then called Love Film) – a postal DVD subscription service that was starting to create a buzz.

Blockbuster, however, lacked the courage to take that choice – for a number of reasons – and they didn't believe that people would step away from the physical DVD to stream films via the internet. Oh, how wrong they were. This lack of courage was a misstep and one that caused their company to fail.

Hindsight makes it easy for us to criticise a company for failing to be courageous, but Blockbuster weren't alone. The photographic company Kodak had a similar problem when they failed to move to digital film, lacking belief in the new form of technology that they themselves had helped to develop. Whether it was a lack of courage to innovate when successful, or a lack of courage to change when struggling. Those that show courage make things happen. So how do we use these lessons to help us deal with those dark clouds on the horizon?

How Can You Use Courage?

If courage can help us survive the difficulties and courage can help us to move forward, then what do we do and how do we make courage our great activator?

If we look at anybody that's done anything of significance, in the whole history of human endeavour, big or small, those people will have been courageous. They might have been at the top – and carried on being at the top. They might have been courageous to carry on and push forward doing something differently, ignoring the 'it ain't broke, don't fix it' mentality. Whatever the situation, courage is the element that gets the stuff moving when you're stuck.

So, when most people think of courage, they might think of it as a 'leap of faith' – a mental image of a bungee or parachute jump. Asking a person out for a date, applying for a job, taking that risk. But Brian Tracy, author of *Eat That Frog!* and *No Excuses!* says that courage has two aspects, and it's the second part of courage that is actually the most important.

To my mind, only 5% of courage is the leap of faith, the jump, the risk taking. Jobs pushing for the iPod, LEGO sticking to the brick. But what follows the deep breath and 'let's go' moment? Tracy suggests that the second part of courage – and the most important – is staying the course. Steve Jobs had to keep going when the iPod didn't immediately gain success. He had to develop iTunes and get the momentum going. He kept on course, and the iPhone followed after. The brand kept evolving, and he showed the courage to stay the course and keep the technology moving forward. The leap of faith is important, but you need to be able to carry on. To keep going. We can all sit down and make the big statement about what we'll do tomorrow – especially after a couple of pints or gin and tonics – but what about the day after that? Because the courageous stay the course.

It's the same principle as resilience. The clouds will come, and you will get knocked down. You show the courage or resilience to get back up (or leap back up), but are you just running into the same problem again? Running into the wall, running into that same fist that knocked you down. Resilience helps us to take a moment to respond and reframe the problem so we can understand it better. Courage helps us to get back up, but also to stay the course once we're up and ready to go.

A huge part of courage is discipline, it's about carrying on with belief. For example, for anyone who likes getting exercise, you might decide to just get fit, or even run a marathon. So, you get up the morning after your decision to get fit. New year, new you. You get your trainers on, you're on the road, you get to the end of the road, and you can't breathe, you need an oxygen tank. Now a lot of people at that point just give up. The New Year's resolutions that don't make it beyond January, well as we all know, are endless. I'm going on a diet. I'm giving up smoking, I'm going to do dry January. I'm going to the gym five times a week. Whatever people decide, the moment they hit the first bit of friction – they stop. Courage is the ability to take the knocks, or those barriers to change, but still carry on.

People mistakenly think success or failure are just up and down lines – smooth and flat pathways to brilliance or the depths of despair. But that's just wrong and a little bit annoying. A life of success is full of ups and downs and all over the place in the hope that we continue to go up. It's like a big game of snakes and ladders. If you're going to do courage properly, there are going to be bumps in the road, there are going to be potholes, there are going to be pitfalls, there may even be extended periods in the valley of despair.

The big question is, do you carry on? That, for me, is the biggest measure of courage. Not the leap of faith. The 'over the top' moment is brave, but thoughtless. It's a simple choice to do or not do, to be or not to be. But once you've made the leap, what's happening? Courage is the ability to leap and then keep moving forward even when the initial decision doesn't seem to be paying dividends straight away. Courage is bigger and much deeper than a single movement or moment. It's about discipline and sacrifice, and Brian Tracy's ability to stay the course. This is COURAGE.

Having contemplated courage both for myself and with others, I felt that there were recurring themes and patterns that kept jumping out at me. My passion was to create a roadmap, or a set of principles that would unlock, simplify or even demystify this prime mover of all virtues. While this list is not exhaustive, I believe it helps people to gain a greater depth of understanding of what this thing called courage is really all about. Having shared this model with numerous teams and individuals over the years, the impact has been extremely positive and so I am always keen to share this learning in the hope that it will help people . . . especially when the clouds come. It was important to me to create a model that was both simple and sticky. So that people can connect with it and remember it. Over a series of months and an organic process, the COURAGE model was born:

C.O.U.R.A.G.E.

C Is for Change

The C in Courage stands for *change*. Our initial idea about courage is our foundation – a 5% leap of faith, and 95% staying the course. That's the road map. The guidelines on which we can show courage, but why do we want to? Even if we want to stick to our original plans and go back to the basics, we still want the clouds to pass us by, we want something to change. So, if you're going to do anything courageous, things are going to have to change. And the problem is – people don't like change. As the saying goes, the only person that likes change is a baby with a dirty nappy. That's probably quite a good analogy for life. Because even some of the most frustrated leaders and people I've come across in life still don't want to change, even though they hate their current reality. They're more wedded to the miserable reality and would rather stay in their little hole of misery.

So, when the clouds come, we show courage by getting our heads around change. As I said in Chapter 1, Einstein's definition of insanity is doing the same things over and over again and expecting different results. You can't do courage if you're just going to do the same things. It's brave to leap back up when you've been knocked down, but not if you keep running into the same thing that knocked you down. And on a more positive note, you can't do courage and stay in your comfort zone. As General Eric Shinseki, retired US Army General says, 'If you don't like change, you'll like irrelevance even less.' Our examples of Blockbuster, Kodak, or even Woolworth's, all tell us something. When things don't go your way, you're going to have to embrace change.

However, a word of caution, because whenever I talk about change, particularly in the realm of courage, I'm reminded of that famous quote, 'All progress is change, but not all change is progress.' Courage is shown through change but change for change's sake is not the same thing. We have to be really selective of what it is we're going to change as we go about being courageous.

I've been really interested in this concept of change over the years and most frequently, it appears as an area of focus and support for leaders with whom I now work. My reading and research have identified the three Cs of change that I consider to be the most significant and meaningful in dealing with this subject.

The first C is to *create* really positive and sustainable change and to do something that will have big impact. This seems easier than it actually is in reality. How many times have you created a change that is both positive and sustainable? Like, 'I'm never eating chocolate ever again' or 'I'm training five times a week from now on' or 'I'm saving £100 every month for the future'? All these changes are positive. They are great in principle but really, are they always sustainable? Likewise, there are times in life when we will also create those small changes that are totally sustainable, but in reality, are they actually making a positive difference? Only having three quarters of the slice of cake instead of the whole thing is sustainable but it won't make the big change dent you're probably hoping for.

Don't just do something that's not going to matter. We aren't talking about flimsy New Year's resolutions that will likely be forgotten on January 4th or 5th. You need to make sure you're creating both positive and sustainable change – and this is a very fine balance.

The second C of change is *challenge*. You've got to challenge the status quo. Challenge the way things are being done. Now you might not change it all, but you should challenge it. This is a direct attempt to stop suffering from analysis paralysis – when your thinking stops you from doing what you need to be doing. Don't wait for the perfect time. Fearing the failure stops you from change and stops you from challenging what is happening. Actually fronting it, eyeballing it, and going for it is a must for successful change.

Creating positive and sustainable change, and challenging the status quo, all take courage. So yes, you guessed it, the third and final aspect of change is part of the bigger whole for *courage*. Change takes courage and courage requires change. And both the leap of faith and staying the course require courage and need change. So, there you have the first step of the COURAGE model – Change.

O Is for Opportunity

When the clouds come, we have to find the courage to be opportunistic. We can easily become laser focused on small details or suffer from blinkered tunnel vision. Our views are often limited to the immediate catastrophe and our emotions relating to that and as a result, we become what sports psychologists refer to as prisoners of our own mind. We see what we want to see. It's a strange kind of comfort to see how terrible a situation is, because at least it's a certainty. But we might not see the opportunity for change. We might not see the sun behind the clouds.

From the outside, leaders like Elon Musk might look decisive, driving forward business using his own ideas with a focused intensity. But many of the talented individuals who work with him will no doubt say his brilliance and annoying quality is because he is the one who dragged disparate, imbalanced, inoperative ideas together and put them into a more coherent form. The courage to be this opportunistic character is key to overcoming your difficulties. It's like the best learners are like magpies, they see the shiny things everywhere and aren't afraid to borrow them. It's taking something and being able to make it work – that's the opportunity. Musk and Jobs alike are criticised for not being the originators or the creators, but they didn't have to be. They were the ones who didn't mind changing stuff. They saw what was available and made the opportunity. You won't always know where the opportunities are going to come from, but you've got to have your eyes open for them.

After the clouds have arrived, some people will attempt to be courageous by setting a fixed goal. Reacting immediately and focusing on one point – getting back up, moving forward, hitting a mark. However, you need to be careful that you're not missing great opportunities that actually could help you reach that goal or maybe take you beyond that goal to something even bigger. We've got to be open to what comes our way. Just like resilience, courage needs a moment to think before responding, to look up and see what's around. It takes courage to be able to wait for that opportunity to come, or at least look for something before jumping onto what could be the nearest 'safe' option.

Curiously, this process is also influenced by the law of attraction. If you're really courageously going forward and you're staying the course towards something, things will come your way that you didn't even dream of. I've had some absolutely fantastic mentors and coaches in my life. They've always said, just keep your eyes open – what we call peripheral vision – because stuff is going to come in from the side and there will be opportunities and some people will miss them. I'm not suggesting we take our eyes off the prize, but I am suggesting that some things that just might not look like they're going to help can actually turn out to be a competitive advantage.

U Is for Understanding

We're expecting change and keeping our eyes open for opportunity. Both of which are processes that give us power and a certain amount of control. They help to give us courage to stay the course. But it's also important to really understand what has happened. Getting back up and moving forward seem so simple, but to make really positive and sustainable changes, you have to have a really deep awareness. And I believe this awareness to be on three levels.

Firstly, are you aware of *you*? What do you really care about? What will you go to the wall for? What are you fired up about? It's about real honesty. Not thin hopes or trying to persuade yourself of something. If you're not fired up about losing weight and you don't really care about it, don't set that as your New Year's resolution just because everyone else is doing it. Do it because you care about it. Otherwise, don't bother. It sounds brutal, but it's about cutting through the emotion and any self-delusion created by the difficulties you're going through and trying to see what is real.

So many people are in careers that they don't really care about. They make decisions that they don't really want because of others, or because of the situation, and then wonder why it doesn't stay the course. If you've not got this self-awareness, how are you going to overcome this current difficulty, let alone any future problems that will inevitably happen?

Self-awareness is why Howard Schultz went back to Starbucks. It's why Steve Jobs went back to Apple. They showed a level of awareness of who they were and what they truly believed in. And also, what they cared about should things go wrong.

Secondly, when you understand yourself, you next need to understand your organisation from a leadership perspective, or your team view. Know what your organisation and your teams stand for. Because you personally might have a burning desire to do something, but the organisation might not be that way. Just because you want to go for a picnic, doesn't mean everyone in your team has bought into the idea of sitting cross-legged eating lukewarm food crouched over on the ground waiting for ants to crawl into your sandwiches.

In leadership terms, if you're going to try and do something courageous and you really believe in it, but that's not what the organisation stands for, then you're a round peg in a square hole. You're in the wrong job. The focus of the individual leader and the organisation have to be aligned. Your understanding and your organisation's understanding of itself have to be in line if you're going to do something courageous. If not, the courageous change won't stay the course. Like the moaning and complaining as you drag your team to an unwanted picnic, you will suffer from so much dissonance within your organisation. You can force them kicking and screaming into a different era, but no one's going to enjoy that and it's not sustainable over the long term. Too much energy is wasted pulling forward, but not enough building.

And finally, the third element – if you can understand yourself, understand your business, or your team, or your circumstances, then you've got to be able to understand the landscape around you. If you want to move forward and change, but the world doesn't need that thing you're offering, do you really need to bother? You're likely to just get knocked back down again. Does your leap of faith go in the right direction? Are you showing courage to stay the course on a pathway that doesn't go anywhere? You need to understand the landscape of what's around you and how your response to this crisis might fit within it.

Returning to Howard Schultz at Starbucks and his passion for what he wanted to create: not coffee, but the coffee experience. He understood what his organisation was and what Starbucks stood for. He understood why he wanted to return to this organisation, his previous home, to create a place for people to go to. And he knew the world needed the 'third space' – home, work, Starbucks – somewhere that could be a mixture of the two. They aligned; therefore, he could do something courageous. He ripped up the script for what Starbucks was.

In short, the understanding works on those three levels, and they have to align. Of course, you can find the courage to take the leap of faith, but if you haven't thought it through and had a real understanding of the three elements, your courageous change won't stay the course. This was the case when creating my own leadership consultancy. My burning passion has always been to help people to develop, I knew my personal purpose in the world. Particularly in the realm of leadership. My family and the people I work with believed that this would make a difference to so many sectors through the work that we do, and I found through conversations with leaders and organisations that there is a real thirst, not just for the work that we do, but for the way we deliver our leadership support. I was therefore hitting those three levels of understanding on my journey. It made sense and I am still compelled to do this work more than ever.

R Is for Resilience

As we explored in the resilience chapter, the boxer Mike Tyson made it clear that 'Everyone has a plan until they get punched in the face.' So it shouldn't be a surprise to know that when you do anything courageous, you are going to take some hits. You may have already been knocked down and be starting to plan your way out of the situation, and you might even get knocked down again.

But it then comes down to, can you get up, and can you get up smarter? This does return to the content in Chapter 1. How do you learn when you're at the bottom? Learn, unlearn, relearn. If you're going to bounce back, you try to bounce back smarter. You show curiosity at the bottom. Resilience is a part of courage. It's the effort. The grit that Dr Angela Duckworth talks about. When you're going through a bad time and you try to understand it and come up with a way through it, you make courageous choices. Effort and resilience keep you courageous. Helping you stay the course and the compound effect of this will create dividends. If you understand why you're putting in the effort, you can be resolute in the way you move through it.

A Is for Action

Talk is cheap and sometimes we have to stop talking and start doing some stuff. This part of courage is less about talking a good game, but more about what you actually can do – big or small. The clouds come and you can discuss the many ways you can avoid, solve or respond to the situation – this book provides many examples of that – but at some point, it's going to be time to just do the courageous thing and actually go for it.

The whole premise of the Nike identity is to 'Just do it'. To just go out and do it. Put your trainers on and run. What's your problem? Just do it, just do it. Even if you only get to the end of the road and stop. This is a key part of courage in response to a crisis. Denis Waitley, sports psychologist and motivational speaker, refers to this as 'action TNT' – acting today and not tomorrow. We can wait for the perfect moment, when the circumstances will be better or more suitable for your plans. Sometimes that perfect opportunity will arise immediately, but more often than not you need to get going now. Start moving forward, as business guru Tom Peters suggests, by being 'action oriented'. In all his studies of excellence, Peters suggests that the best people to resolve issues, resist crises and achieve excellence are action oriented. If you're going to do something courageous, you're going to have to act at some point. It doesn't have to be grand. It doesn't have to be a leap of faith without further planning, but you do have to move.

A by-product of when we go out and do stuff and take the leap of faith is that every now and again we're going to fail. Of course we are. This is like a sidebar to action where you're going to have to understand that everything you act on is not all going to come out rosy. There are going to be times of failure. But you still have to be courageous and act. And as Matthew Syed talked about in his book, *Black Box Thinking*, it's the learning that we get from the failures that is really important. If we act, we're going to fail.

However, be sure that it is the action that is critical. We must make a start. We must overcome that initial inertia if we are to gain momentum and do courage.

G Is for Goals

The more I consider courage and those leaders and individuals that show it, the more I realise that they have an ultimate endpoint. They don't just decide to do something great and go. And they don't just get up from a knock-down and decide to do better. They have a goal. A goal based on something they will have learnt from the failure, or from their previous experiences.

Now the goal might change over time, but they're always going towards something and it's always big. Elon Musk has decided he wants to create space travel for everyone (and you can see his very public failures along the way). These people are going out and they have got what Jim Collins refers to as BHAGs: big, hairy, audacious goals. Very stereotypical of a business mindset, but don't let it put you off. The point is this: if you're going to do something courageous, where are you going with it? Don't just randomly suggest to do something fabulous. It's the perfect time to focus and think. Really set that kind of goal and vision for the future that says this is what I want to do. I want to change the world in this way. What's the impact of this going to be?

Steve Jobs wanted to make people's worlds better, and the iPhone arguably does that. Some would argue that it doesn't, but the courageous decision to not follow the previous technological innovations has really streamlined a lot of things for society if it's used in the right way. Consider that a young person with a phone can set up a business or be able to study without previous financial and technological restrictions. Courage means having those big goals. We can't do courage unless we're going somewhere with it. What are we trying to do here? What's the aspiration? Too many people have an average aspiration: 'I'm just going to go in and do that'. But if you say to people, 'Have you got average aspirations?' They'll say, 'Absolutely not. Categorically not. How dare you even suggest that I have!' You want amazing aspirations so have the courage to set amazing goals.

E Is for Engagement

In our search for that courage, we come to the final piece of the jigsaw. Everything in this book is about how to respond and deal with the clouds that come in life. It's about helping you as an individual to get up and move forward by yourself, as an organisation, or as a family. And that's the key part of courage – you don't need to do anything courageous alone.

As an Everton fan it is extremely difficult for me to praise Liverpool FC in any way. But over the last few years their style of play and performances have been eye-catching in the world of sport. Under the leadership of Jürgen Klopp they have won numerous trophies and become known for their fast, expansive, and innovative style of play. But Klopp wasn't on his own – he had a team of people behind him. They were there to help him make his courageous goals something that could be acted upon. I was fortunate enough to be asked to attend his induction into the League Managers Association Hall of Fame. And when asked about what the secret to his success was, Klopp pointed to his whole team in the audience, and it was clear that he was aware that their success was not down to just one person. This is true level 5 leadership. I believe that courageous acts do not have to be done alone.

More often than not if you're trying to do something courageous alone, initiate change on your own, then it won't work as effectively as when you have a team of people around you. You've got to get a group of good people that share your 'why'. It's not that you cannot do it alone, and it isn't even that other people are always helpful, but if we're looking for courage to make change and to move forward, then a group of people can make it easier, better, and can help that positivity last longer.

You want people to help you look for the opportunities, to understand what's going on, to help you be resilient when those tough times come. People that are willing to put themselves out there, while working towards your goal. It's the teamwork stuff that really matters. The engagement bit, whilst it's at the end of COURAGE, potentially it should go at the beginning. Because you're definitely making it harder for yourself if you haven't got a good set of people who are going to go on that journey with you. Have you heard of the saying, 'We walk at the pace of the five people we spend most of our time with'? So, if we spend our working or personal life surrounded by negative voices, cynical voices, indifferent voices, then that's what we start to become. Both positive engagement and negative engagement will have an impact on us. And when the clouds come, we don't need any more negativity.

Easier said than done, but if you're going to do courage, you need to surround yourselves with people who believe in what you believe in and who are going to understand the things that you want to do. That might be harder in a personal situation, but you know the friends that lift you up and the friends that sadly drag you down. In an organisation, that's where the recruitment and the leadership are really important. In both cases, we do have to be selective about our own personal environments in our life, but that's how we do courage. You've got to check your environment.

That's not about saying to someone I can't be your friend anymore because you don't share my goals, but it is about limiting the impact that their negative influence may have. Getting knocked down can feel incredibly lonely. Getting back up doesn't have to be. We literally stand on the shoulders of giants that have been before us – again it's a cliché, but it is true.

Every one of us has benefited from someone showing courage in the past, maybe someone personally in your life or someone culturally inspiring. If you're going to do courage well, don't try and do it on your own. Anyone that's climbed Mount Everest knows about the team of people behind it. Maybe not on the climb with them, but getting them fit, helping them eat well, bandaging up swollen feet, etc. Whenever you hear about somebody who has achieved something great the first thing they do, if they're a great leader or person, is talk about all the other people who made it possible. It's always a team thing. Engagement is at the heart of courage.

Courage to Listen

Combining resilience and courage allows you to do one thing we can all do when we're feeling alone – we can listen. You've probably been punched out of your comfort zone and it's tempting to run back into that place of safety but take advantage of the moment. You don't have to crawl back into your armchair or hide in the life you already have because that will inevitably lead to the same problems recurring again and again.

That's why it's important to listen. It does require some bravery to jump up and run headlong back into the life that knocked you down, but it's even more courageous to pause and consider what is happening. It shows resilience and courage to pause, think and listen to what is around. Simply standing up, taking a breath, thinking about things, starting to make a move forward, looking around for people to work with. It makes everything easier. It's not so abrupt. It doesn't drain so much energy. It's got to be more incremental; it's got to be a little bit more thoughtful.

It sounds ridiculous but if you're hungry, you don't eat a whole cow, do you? You eat a burger. So, it's about you trying to make a big leap palatable, easy to swallow, bite-sized, chunking it down, whatever and however that helps you manage it. Because that's the reality for most of us after the clouds come. We might not feel like we're Steve Jobs or Elon Musk or Howard Schultz, but that doesn't mean we don't want things to be better. It doesn't mean we don't aspire to big goals.

In *Courage Goes to Work,* Bill Treasurer says there are three types of courage. Try courage – which is to have a go at new things. Trust courage – where you rely on others. And then there's tell courage – where you speak your mind. These are the different ways in which you can show courage in small incremental and manageable ways. Courage isn't facing an unknown and not being scared or intimidated. Courage is knowing the storm is outside, but still putting on your waterproofs and heading out there.

Personally, I've lived most of my career in a really safe, public sector job. Challenging, absolutely. Heartbreaking and life-affirming in equal measure but my job itself was pretty safe, so far as jobs go. Then the clouds came, and the situation changed and suddenly I had to set up on my own. Scared to death of the impact on my family and finances, but in a position where I had to saddle up anyway. A courageous leap of faith that has tested my resilience and brought me to the point at which I can now share these experiences.

Winston Churchill said, 'Courage is what it takes to stand up and speak.' That seems clear and obvious to anyone in these current times. Speaking out against the most obvious wrongs and incivility within the modern world – I think everyone understands that. But 'courage is also what it takes to sit down and listen'. It takes courage to sit and hear the truth about your situation, to sit and get the feedback on your performance or behaviour, to sit and hear critical comments made. No one likes to hear negativity, but if you show the courage to listen, really listen, to what the world is saying about your situation, you can gain so much.

People think courage is purely about what you do, how you speak, what you work towards and how you get everyone around moving. Actually, it's also very much about the quiet moments of courage when you sit there and you listen. You listen to what you're saying to yourself. And you listen to what may have been said. You know, you're not going to agree with it all. I'm not even saying you need to take it all on board. But you've given yourself a chance to listen. Because if you don't really sit and listen to yourself and others, I don't think you can really understand yourself and others. That's true courage.

Chapter 3

THE POWER OF UNCER- TAINTY

Have you ever come across the quote; 'Better to be a dog in times of tranquillity, than a human in times of chaos'? It's an expression now more commonly misused and changed to what is regarded as the well-known 'curse' – 'May you live in interesting times.' And I am sure for most people, this pretty much sums up the feelings about 2020–2021. Whatever people might say about the pandemic and everything this entailed, including its several lockdowns, I think it's fair to suggest that we have all experienced every single emotion possible.

It was a year which saw highs, it saw lows and it saw pretty much everything in between. As the year went on, it was the unknowing and the uncertainty that became, unusually, the one consistency for us all. It didn't matter who you were, what job you had, where you lived, what friendship groups you were in, what your talents or interests were – there was a sense of unknowing and uncertainty amongst everyone.

Whenever we find ourselves looking in the rear-view mirror of a past year, many different emotions can emerge, and they will be dependent entirely upon what that year brought us. And consequently, that view might not provide us with any confidence, or hope for the upcoming year.

While we all do this, we should try to spend more of our time looking forward, on that unknown and untravelled road ahead. Which oftentimes is much easier said than done. Coming out of lockdown 3, I think the one word which accurately summed up all of our situations was uncertainty. A time also when we were all looking for the things that would bring us back to that sense of 'normal'. To that sense of certainty, sureness and security that we may have felt, pre-pandemic.

With hindsight, I'm just not sure that searching for that elusive 'normal' was actually ever going to work. And this is not about me being negative or a doom-monger, but instead it's a realisation, reflecting on where we have all just been, and coming to the understanding that we have to instead learn to deal with the certainty of uncertainty and all that this entails.

Moving out of 2020 into 2021 was what can only be described as a mixed moment for our pandemic nation. The vaccines were rolling out thick and fast. Christmas and New Year 2020 plans had been kyboshed. A third national lockdown was in force. The usual mix of January hope and despair was ever present: resolution and realisation, seasonal sadness, and a sense of optimism. The latter as you well know isn't a new phenomenon, but during that period, it certainly felt more acute. It felt like there was an overwhelming sense of uncertainty following the previous 12 months.

What Is Uncertainty to You?

To most people, it is fair to say that uncertainty equals the unknown. In coaching and development sessions if I ask the question 'what is uncertainty?' people respond that it's anxiety, nervousness, worry, being unsure and feeling unsafe. We feel like we live in a very VUCA world – volatile, uncertain, complex, ambiguous – and so when asked that question, we seem to just list lots and lots of negative words with negative connotations, clearly illustrated in the points above. And that seems relatively normal. Due to a sense of security, we fear the unknown for instinctual prehistoric reasons. We create anxiety and fear around the unknown in order for us to remain safe and secure. But conversely, this unending conversation about uncertainty seems to create the very opposite of feeling secure. Instead, this view of uncertainty in relation to anxiety can have a negative impact on those around you, and of course on yourself. The lack of certainty around whatever issue or problem you're facing becomes the bigger problem, rather than the fear of the actual future problem itself. That underlying feeling of the 'bad' that looms in the distance. The lack of surety in our footsteps, the general and overwhelming feeling of unease – these are all things that start to dominate our thoughts. But how we do we overcome this? How do we move forward? When the clouds come we have already seen that we need to reframe our concepts of resilience and courage so that we can get up and keep going, but how do we reframe our concept of uncertainty?

To help yourself and others around you in uncertainty, I believe you need to understand three uncertainty dynamics. This is particularly pertinent to leaders because, obviously, they're managing and leading people every day so of course they need to be aware of how other people are feeling and what they are facing. However, it is something we can all apply and use to support ourselves or others through any difficult time.

Worrying about Coffee

Firstly, people worry. It's a primary dynamic in uncertainty and I think there's been more than a lot of worry this past year. The word 'worry' comes from the Greek word which means divided mind, and that, for me, sums up exactly what happens to us when we are caught in this place. It literally divides your mind. You should be in one place but your mind is over in another place some of the time and so you can end up never properly in focus.

You can't have that laser focus because you're worried and it's dividing your thoughts. When you're at work, you're thinking about your family and worrying about them. When you're with your family, you're worrying about work and you're not quite ever where you are meant to be, which is a major problem. This isn't just a pandemic problem, but it's definitely an uncertainty dynamic which causes us immediate difficulty. Like the old saying goes, 'Worry is a bit like sitting in a rocking chair – it gives you something to do, but it doesn't get you very far.' There is nothing productive about worrying.

Yet while we all may know that worrying is pointless we still all do it. So how do you break out of this habit and free yourself from the worrying mindset? It's tough. I remember being with a really good mentor of mine and he was talking about this very thing. We were in a coffee shop, and I was worrying about something or other. And he said, 'You need to think about worry like that cup of coffee.' I was waiting for him to give me something profound about coffee and patience, or beans and water transforming it into something better, but he didn't say anything. After a while, I asked him what he was talking about? And he said, 'No, no. Think about that cup of coffee. If you picked up that cup of coffee and you lifted it out in front of you, how long do you think you could hold it up for?'

My slightly puzzled response: 'I have no idea and quite frankly I don't know if I care.'

'No, no. Come on. How long do you think you could hold it up for?'

'I don't know, like five minutes or something. I like to think I'm reasonably fit.'

'Yeah, but you couldn't hold it up like that forever, could you?'

'Well, no.' (With a possible eye roll.)

'And that's what worry is like. You have to put it down sometime. You can't hold on to it forever, otherwise you'll start to get very tired as a result of having to hold on to it.'

So my first question about worry is – what is it that we're worried about?

Right now, your response might be, 'How long have you got?' Health, work, the kids' future, climate change – in these particularly difficult times we're worrying about what we might lose, that kind of worst-case scenario. Our minds have an ability to catastrophise. It's always to the negative. We're not worrying that too many good things will happen. We know that a loss has a much bigger impact on us than a gain when we're worrying. So, for example, when you lose a £20 note, what do you do? Well, you spend ages looking for it. Ridiculous amounts of time. Where did I put it? When did I last have it? Did I definitely not put it in my wallet? You're almost at the point where you're going to slash your sofa up to find that £20 note.

But let's compare that with when we find a £20 note. When you actually find £20 that you weren't expecting to find, it was in your wallet and you hadn't noticed it. You'd forgotten about it in that little jeans pocket. It was hidden away in the drawer. You just say, 'Oh, YES! I've found £20.' You'll be happy. But you're not bothered to the same extent. The energy you expend is much less and that's because the loss, or fear of loss, has a bigger impact on us psychologically than a gain will have. That's something I think we've got to be aware of when we're talking about uncertainty.

From Worry to Fear

Moving to the second uncertainty dynamic is a logical progression for many psychologists who say that if you don't deal with the worry, it then moves to becoming fear. For many in recent years that has been a quick progression. People have been fearful, some may have not dealt with the worry, but some people would rightly ask what exactly is it that people are fearful of?

Again, from reading and observing, I think what people are actually fearing is failure. We've talked about that for years. I've been somebody that's talked about this fear of failure for as long as I can remember. There's a fear we have of failing at life, or in work, or wherever it might be. For example, if you're divorced, you might feel (wrongly) that you've failed in your personal life and as a result of this you then fear the view that you're a failure.

I was reading an article by leadership guru Seth Godin once, and within this he stated that it's not failure that we fear. As human beings we know we're going to fail and actually, we know we need to fail to get better. It's in our earliest social development: How do you learn to walk? You fall over. How do you learn to ride a bike? You fall off. Godin says it's not failure that we're fearful of, but the criticism that's connected to the failure.

Fear of failure is a strange concept because the consequence of falling down, tripping up, dropping something, any embarrassing moment is different when you're on your own, to when you have an audience. I was talking to my good mate Paul McGee – The SUMO Guy – about this very subject once. He was saying that, for him, this is so true. He said, 'I can't park my car. I can't reverse park to save my life. And I know I'm going to mess it up when I do it. But if I'm going out for dinner with my family, I will drop them off at the restaurant and drive a ludicrous amount of time and distance away from where I should be just so that I can park with nobody around. If the family's not in the car, I can still fail but I don't want the people standing, pointing at me, ribbing me about it. It's the criticism that's connected to the failure.'

So is it the fear of failure that is consuming us now? I definitely think that people are aware that it's not been the easiest of years for anyone. But are we actually more fearful of failing? Possibly not, because we can get our heads around that concept. The idea that is constant within modern society is comparison and how others view us. Even in this time of collective uncertainty and worry, we still find the fear of criticism or judgement from others is prevalent. And you can see how that anxiety is building because of the endless uncertainty presented to us by our current circumstances.

When the clouds come, you are faced with uncertainty – the worry, then the fear of failure – what's going to happen? And what if I get it wrong? Or respond in the wrong way? Now, those two are bad enough for even the most resilient of us, but if you add uncertainty dynamic number three, then we really feel like we're up against it.

Bye-Bye Comfort Zone

Like all good things, uncertainty dynamics come in threes and alongside worry and fear of failure, when you're in a period of uncertainty, you're completely outside of your comfort zone. Did anyone feel totally normal or at ease in 2020? Did anyone think, oh well, we'll just do what we've always done?

The phrase 'unprecedented' has been a defining comment during this pandemic. Everybody has felt outside of their comfort zone. And this is a problem for humans because we like to be in control. We like to know. We like things to be predictable. Those three things define what uncertainty does not and this is pretty damaging and pretty difficult for us to deal with. Not only for ourselves and for the people around us, but within our businesses and as leaders particularly, this is where people are currently. They might be suffering a range of different feelings around uncertainty, less or more negative, less or more worried or fearful, or less or more out of control. However, we're all suffering this global uncertainty, and it's an important thing to bear in mind and reflect upon for yourself and those around you, whether the clouds have come or not.

I'm aware of how gloomy and depressing that sounds and right now I imagine you'll be concerned that I haven't provided a positive solution to these uncertainty dynamics, and I haven't brushed them aside with a set of logical and practical processes. But just be patient. The first thing to acknowledge is the uncertainty of the world – to really look it in the eye. We have to be aware of it – really aware of it – to be able to do anything about it. We can flip our thinking about uncertainty, but we have to see what we're up against first – worry, fear and a lack of comfort zone.

Time to Flip

Now here comes the good stuff – each of those uncertainty dynamics has a counterpoint. A method to flip or change your perspective to counteract what will undoubtedly be an energy-draining and self-defeating experience. Viewing uncertainty negatively does not benefit us. It's understandable to feel negative, and it's inevitable that we will experience uncertainty, but it doesn't have to be combined.

Firstly, I believe uncertainty is where innovation lives. Whenever you do anything great, you rip up a script. Starting a business, moving jobs, moving home, starting a family, beginning a hobby, whatever the new thing is – you have to move to uncertainty to begin. Nothing innovative or new is ever predictable and certain, but that's actually when we make those biggest strides and feel positive. This is when we reimagine ourselves and what we do. This is when we do something completely fantastic like Steve Jobs and the iPod.

Great innovation never comes from a place of certainty. The fact that it's not been done before is really big. Of course, you can't become remarkable by doing what other people have done. You have to do something new and you have to do something great and that is not going to come from a place of control and complete certainty.

This is a time, I think, where a lot of people have innovated. It might have been dressed up as survival (our negative language changes our perspective), but we've all done new things. We've innovated in our work practices and our family lives. Did we ever imagine homeschooling on such a mass scale? And think how innovative all the teachers have been to create and deliver lessons and resources virtually in these 'unprecedented' times. Will we all go back to working in offices and commuting to work? Will our working hours be more flexible for parents and non-parents alike? Across the world, the response to our uncertain situation has led to some seriously wonderful innovation, and innovation is a positive.

Secondly, uncertainty should not be a surprise to us as humans. Innovation is where we learn and grow towards our potential, and if you really think about the whole of our first 20 years on the planet, everything is ambiguous, and nothing is certain. Growing up and developing as a human child means encountering the new and the novel every single day. Each child's 'firsts' are 'unprecedented'. First tooth, first solids, first step, first day at school – everything is uncertain and new, and we deal with it. When you're going to school every day, you don't know what you're going to be doing in your lessons. You don't know whether you're going to be able to manage it, but you go in. These are the times when we really learn and grow because it isn't certain and we don't know whether we can do it and we push ourselves to new levels. Humans are far more adaptable and used to uncertainty than we give ourselves credit for.

In a more structured environment, it's like training at the gym. When you go in, you don't know whether you can lift that weight, but you push yourself to the point of failure and that's how you learn and you grow and you get stronger. This is a time when actually, in these moments of uncertainty, we get probably our greatest learning and our greatest growth.

Prior to Roger Bannister running the four-minute mile, everybody had said it was impossible. Biologically, psychologically, physiologically, you couldn't do it. But he did it, because he believed he could, and he pushed himself during that place of uncertainty to do the four-minute mile. And then, funnily enough, when he had done it, everybody's response was that of 'Well, that's the end of the story'. But it wasn't. And that is because of the shift of the four-minute mile now being a certainty. Within three or four weeks of him doing it, other people also did it because that thing, that impossible thing – the four-minute mile – then became certain. Everybody knew they had a chance to do it. It could now be done.

Moving an uncertainty to a certainty is a strange phenomenon, but it's become so commonplace that we often don't see it. This year alone I think there are lots of examples of people feeling like they could never do something, then doing it, and then it becoming the new normal.

In times of certainty, sat in our comfort zones, people make decisions based on avoiding fear or worry, or simply seeking familiar habit – 'I would never work from home'. Well, guess what? We actually did manage to work from home and some of us preferred it, or at least realised they could do it quite well, leading to the option of flexible working, or part-time in the office. Uncertainty taught us many things, some innovative, but some as part of a continuous evolution of our situation. If there's no uncertainty, we're probably not going to learn and grow towards our potential.

In short, uncertainty is not all bad news. If we could frame it as 'uncertainty is where innovation lives', then we might feel a little less negative towards it. It's the time when we can break free from the chances of certainty and do things differently without judgement and derision. Uncertainty can be where we learn and grow towards our potential.

Finally – and I'm aware that this might irritate some people – the thing about uncertainty is that it can actually be quite exhilarating. Now, bear with me. I'm not saying I'm an adrenalin junkie. In actual fact, you would not find me putting a big elastic band around my ankle and jumping off a bridge, or out of a plane. And I don't care what the stats say about safety. That level of uncertainty is not for me and I'm not going to do it. But despite this admission, uncertainty is still a thrill, a source of excitement, a positive energy.

Think about travel for a moment. This first thought many of us may have had after lockdown is to perhaps book a holiday. To go somewhere new and different and leave our comfort zones – and embrace some uncertainty. Visiting that new place. Trying that new drink by the pool. Exploring a new culture. We like the exhilaration of what could happen – the possible. It gives us hope.

Probably the arena I know better than any other is elite sport. You talk to any top-level athlete, any top-level coach, any top-level strength and conditioner, they don't want to be in the easy comfortable games where they're battering a team 60-nil in rugby or 6-nil in football. The one-sided victory. The easy win. They want to play on the big occasion which is riddled with uncertainty, the cup final or the international game where nobody knows what the result's going to be. This could be a defining moment. They want to play in the world cup final against one of the best teams to test themselves because they find it exhilarating and exciting to be in that moment of uncertainty.

Reframing Uncertainty – The Way Forward

I think reframing uncertainty is a powerful thing to do. Uncertainty is not all bad news. However, the first initial response is the unknown – the anxious, the ambiguous, the volatile, the uncertain. That gives people worry. And then people are worried about what they might lose. People do fear the failure and all the criticism, and people do feel completely out of the comfort zone. But imagine if we flip the thinking and, as we've said, uncertainty's where innovation lives. This is our time to innovate. Let's look at it, let's reframe it totally differently. If we accept that uncertainty is where we learn and grow and we head towards our potential, then uncertainty can be quite exciting and quite exhilarating. That's the framing of it.

Realistically, we know that uncertainty is not something we'd probably ask for. But it's there already in smaller or larger doses. We simply hide it under our various ways to find comfort and security. So, for me – like you – when those uncertain clouds have come, I've not liked it. I've not been feeling like,

'Oh, great. Uncertainty.' But the more I've been aware of uncertainty, the more I have been able to explore it in my own mind's eye and think, 'Well, actually, I could do something different, innovation. I am going to get better as a result of this. What could I learn? What could I do?'

Even before the first lockdown when I started working online it felt like a nightmare. Even the small things were getting to me – I couldn't get the mouse to work because of the settings on my Mac. I felt awkward delivering everything on video calls and I just couldn't work out how best to do it. I was trying to hold on to my previous ways of doing things and it wasn't working. I was feeling more negative about staying in my comfort zone and holding on to what I knew how to do. So, I forced myself to do it differently – to innovate – but actually to go back to some older previous skills and practices I had forgotten I had even once used. The energy and exhilaration I found from finding a way through the negativity to try the uncertain things was palpable. I loved it. I enjoyed the wrestle. Trying to solve the problems. And as humans, I think we *can* enjoy it. Maybe more at the end of things and maybe not when we're in the middle of the difficulty, but we can enjoy it.

Just like going on holiday – we deliberately choose to take a very small number of belongings in an awkward-sized case, cram ourselves into tiny uncomfortable seats to sit for hours of travel, to end up in a place we don't know, don't speak the language, or know where or even what to eat. We literally choose to leave behind everything comfortable and familiar each time we book that week in the sun. But we love it. Just because we reframe uncertainty as excitement when we go on holiday. It's that simple. We reframe the same thing in a positive light.

As humans, it isn't just travel that makes us reframe uncertainty as a positive. When you're watching a detective programme on TV, when you're watching a horror movie, when you jump on a roller coaster at a theme park – you're choosing to be scared. You're choosing to be a little bit frightened. You're choosing uncertainty for fun. A lot of people seek out all those things: the thrill, the jumps, the shivers, but there is always a safe framework of understanding underneath it. In these moments, we pick out fear, we pick out uncertainty.

What's the difference between these moments of uncertainty and the arrival of those storm clouds? Maybe it is something to do with choice. Uncertainty is horrible when it feels like it is being done to us. When we feel powerless to control it. But we literally run towards uncertainty when we can choose it. We all seem very brave, and we seek uncertainty for that adrenaline, thrill, excitement. People get buzzed about going on a first date or whatever it might be. We choose to take those risks. How do you frame uncertainty in the same way that we sometimes want to look positively at risk? Because risk is the same principle, isn't it?

How do you frame that uncertainty in a choosing way? Uncertainty, when we're in it, it's just happening to us. We may, for example, have no faith in what the government is saying, we've no faith that the people around us are going to behave appropriately. So, we get very, very, negative. It's all uncertain. So how can we find a positive reframing to uncertainty without just hiding in our comfort zones?

In all cases of uncertainty, a positive reframing means you are balancing out the wins versus the losses. There's no safety net on a first date but we seek out that uncertainty with the balance between what could go wrong versus what could go right. And I think it is experience that allows us to have that awareness. We gain balance by knowing the wins and the losses. When we gain perspective, we are looking at the risks a little more objectively. Whether it's about getting older and wiser, or you simply gain more perspective from experience. But for me, what is really, really powerful is that because I've been through those uncertain moments, when negative things have happened to me – and I'm not saying I was on top of everything – but I had the belief that I could find a way through this because I've been in really difficult moments before and I've navigated it.

If we can stop and connect it back to past experiences and remember that actually there are some things that are powerful about this. This isn't just happening to me. It's happening to everyone. It's not the whole of my life that's a complete car crash and actually, this won't last forever. Remembering the 3Ps from Chapter 1: the personalisation, the pervasiveness and the permanence in this difficulty are vital. When you want to flip from the uncertainty dynamics, these are really key concepts to learn and overcome.

Fear Focusing

The first uncertainty flipping skill is what I call fear focusing. Something that Tim Ferriss calls 'fear setting'. The idea is this: we have to go towards that thing that really scares us. Jim Collins talks about the moment you 'confront the brutal facts'. Whatever you're uncertain about, you have to eyeball the thing. Or 'Feel the fear and do it anyway', the Susan Jeffers stuff. But what we very often do in practice is reel away from that thing that's difficult.

Some people absolutely swear by the exhilarating effect of a cold shower in the morning. For others, the very thought of it is preposterous and you shiver before even stepping one foot inside the shower. You don't want to go towards the cold because you know it's not going to be very pleasant. But once you're in it, and you've got used to it, it's actually a really exhilarating feeling. I'm not suggesting going towards everything you fear creates exhilaration, but it does with a cold shower. The idea of fear focusing is to go towards your absolute worst-case scenario. What is the worst-case scenario for you when the clouds come? What is the worst that uncertainty can bring?

When you've worked out what it is – go towards it. Front up to it. That process in itself is quite empowering. Just staring down at your worse outcome and considering how you can deal with this bleak scenario. In most cases, there will be a solution, a response, a way forward. In fact, I would go further to say that in any scenario there will always be a solution and a way forward; there has to be. Time to create a plan – just one side of A4 paper – a plan to overcome this worst-case scenario. This is all part of fear focusing. Tell me what you'd do? How you would do it? When you would do it? And why you would do it? A very basic action plan for slaying the dragon. Once you've done that, it's one of the weirdest, yet most fascinating feelings you can have.

A strange realisation that you have a strategy for the worst-case scenario – and then you put it in a box and don't look at it again.

You want to feel your shoulders drop, the tension release. If that is the worst-case scenario, and nobody dies as a result, then is it really that bad after all? Suddenly, everybody's shoulders drop. You see the fear, you front it, you create the plan. You put the plan away and that plan is always there and there's some level of security that we get to say to ourselves, 'Well, do you know what? If the brown smelly stuff hits the fan, I know exactly what I'm going to do.' That's how fear focusing flips uncertainty and replaces worry and fear with a sense of something known.

A terrible known scenario you've written down is easier to deal with than an unknown possibility. Psychologists have been talking about this for years, but here's the final thought on fear focusing – how often does your worst-case scenario actually happen? Not very often. This doesn't mean that bad things don't happen, but it does mean that we create and catastrophise. Fear of the uncertainty makes us fixate on what rarely ever happens – the worst case. And if it does actually happen, we still have a plan in a box to help counter it and deal with the leftovers. The reality is that fear focusing literally gives people the power back in their lives. It makes us confront uncertainty and realise that often, it isn't as big and frightening as we may have first thought.

Ambiguity Tolerance

The second uncertainty flipping skill is ambiguity tolerance. Basically, it's exactly what it says on the tin: getting used to ambiguity. Tolerance for change and uncertainty are key, and we've probably developed this skill more than we think during the last year or two. It's not a particularly sexy concept, but we're not very good at ambiguity. We try to keep our house at the same temperature. We like to sit in the same chairs. We like the shower in a certain position. We try and create as much comfort as possible. By reinforcing our comfort zone, we make the impact of uncertainty bigger and more powerful, and this makes us less able to handle ambiguity. And the solution is to train yourself to deal with ambiguity.

Imagine taking a different route to work. People absolutely hate doing that. Take a different route. Sit on a different seat on the bus. Park in a different spot. Have a different sandwich for lunch. All of this will feel weird. Even the thought of it will be making some of you cringe a little bit, but it works. It feels weird, but it's a great way to use ambiguity to improve the way we deal with levels of uncertainty.

I always liked the idea of cold showers because of what it does to people physiologically and psychologically. No one really wants to have a cold shower but still I persuaded myself to do it. For the last two years, I have a regular warm shower and then I make myself do at least a minute in a cold shower. It's horrible to experience, but it's about building my ambiguity tolerance. I think human beings can build up and prepare themselves for ambiguity like training for a marathon. This is like training for life and training for the uncertainty in life. Build up your levels of ambiguity. Get used to those moments that you don't quite know.

Like many people in the last couple of years, as I mentioned earlier, I had to move a lot of my work from in-person to virtual and it wasn't easy. But I embraced the ambiguity and deliberately made myself do loads of online stuff. I wasn't always enjoying it, but it made me more comfortable with uncertainty. Across the world, everyone has had to get used to a 'new normal' and that in itself is building your ambiguity tolerance. We've adapted to home-schooling, we've adapted to working from home, we've adapted to not seeing our families and friends. Everything has been in a state of uncertainty and ambiguity, and we've been working our ambiguity tolerance harder than we might realise. We still might feel beleaguered and complain about it all, but we're becoming experts at ambiguity.

Nurture a Growth Mindset

The third uncertainty flipping skill comes from Carol Dweck's research on mindset in her wonderful book *Mindset: The new Psychology of Success*. If you have a fixed mindset in a place of uncertainty, well you can be pretty damn sure that you're going to come a cropper. It's very likely you're going to fall flat on your face. Growth mindset on the other hand isn't about a single goal, it's about a pervading attitude to everything you do. Everyone is in the same boat at the moment and our goals may be similar, but we need to look at growth – growth lasts forever.

Anyone can hit a goal and still do badly, or similarly we can miss a goal but do well. In sport, teams can play brilliantly and lose, or they can play poorly and win. Goals aren't therefore always a real or true test of development and progress. Human progress is about growth. It's about the amount of effort we're putting in. It's the idea of – are we getting better? It's okay that I haven't done that yet. I think explaining growth mindset and growth versus goals is really powerful in places of uncertainty because I think we all feel we can do something about our own growth. We can all do something about our effort. We can all do something about our learning. We are in control of that, but we might not be in control of every goal we set or outcome we desire. Fixed mindset means the goal becomes the absolute – we meet it, we succeed; we miss, we're a failure. Life is never that simple. We get knocked down – that's it, it's over. Well, it isn't, is it?

We don't do this enough in life. We fix our minds. This is who I am. This is what I do. I live within this comfort zone here. Well, actually, you don't. Your position in this world is not absolute. It's not final – good or bad. It's not fixed. You could go outside your comfort zone and why not? What if your comfort zone is shaken by the pandemic? What if you miss your goal because of circumstances beyond your control? A fixed mindset frustrates and means you have already failed before you started. A growth mindset suggests it's a setback on the way to something bigger. It happened, but time didn't stop. You're still rolling forward. Sometimes up, and sometimes down, but always forward.

Certainty Anchors

My fourth uncertainty flipping skill comes from a book called *Uncertainty* by Jonathan Fields. He says that what we need in moments of uncertainty is to remember our 'certainty anchors'. If you stop and look at your life – what are you certain about? You're clearly uncertain about a huge number of things, but what are the immovable things you can control? It's a strange thought, but a great exercise to do. I'm certain about what time I can get up. I'm certain about my morning routine. I can be certain about what I eat. I can be certain about this piece of work and this piece of work and this part of the job and this aspect of the business. When I actually had ranked them all up and done a list, I was probably certain of about 85% of my life. It was the 15% that was giving me the worry, fear and out-of-comfort-zone stuff.

But when I put it on a list and I wrote it down, I realised that these 'certainty anchors' are what's going to give me the stuff I need to be able to function. I'm not going to go into fight, freeze or flight mode. I have a solid base of things that will help me approach the uncertainty with a growth mindset. I am certain on these things and I'm going to keep putting the effort in on those uncertain things.

Every time I've done this exercise with an individual or a team, it has been a penny-dropping moment. When you stop and think about it, you're actually in control of a hell of a lot of your life. A big majority of what you do is more or less certain. It doesn't stop the worry, but the worry is often smaller than you might first think. If you can concentrate on those 'certainty anchors' they can give you a feeling of control that uncertainty steals from you. Uncertainty comes from a tiny percentage of your day to day, and that is more manageable to cope with.

Choose Option B

The fifth and final uncertainty flipping skill is the choice of option B. Directly building on Sheryl Sandberg's wonderful book *Option B*, I think that in moments of uncertainty, it's good to step back from it and ask yourself the question – what mindset am I approaching with here? It takes some strength and requires a growth mindset, but in this place of uncertainty, am I looking at opportunities? What could I do? How could it be done? Where could we go? The alternative is the catastrophic fixed mindset: What are the obstacles? What can't I do? What happened to the life I used to have?

It sounds naïve and simplistic but you have to create an option B. It's not about good or bad, success or failure, it just is. A lot of people this year have had to create an option B. They simply couldn't do life as they did before. You can sit there and have a little pity party for yourself but remember that this is simply your emotions catastrophising and it doesn't get you anywhere.

During lockdown I couldn't travel for work or appear in person at events, and it felt like everything might stop. When you have a family to provide for, bills to pay, a roof to keep over your head and you're not sure what you're dealing with, then it is a worrying time. But option B was there – I could do more online stuff. I could make the virtual world of work, work for me. I didn't know how at first. I did make many mistakes. But the business changed, and my work changed with it. Option B was a mindset. It's the opportunity versus the obstacles. If you start obsessing over the obstacles, you're going to soon find yourself in a downward spiral. If instead you start thinking, what are the opportunities here? then that is going to be a more exciting and positive experience. The energy feeds into how you feel and what you do.

This even goes for those very dire circumstances, including bereavement and loss. When Sheryl Sandburg is talking about the death of a loved one and how to deal with grief, she mentions that while you may not be able to have Option A, you can create an Option B. Of course, death is finite, and nothing will be the same after it, but with even this process or example, there can be an Option B. You absolutely cannot change the diagnosis/prognosis or situation, so you have to move forward with something different. It is one of the most serious examples of how you turn the initial response of fear of the future into recreating the life that goes on. Uncomfortable – certainly. Painful – definitely. Unavoidable – absolutely. Uncertainty in life can still be flipped on its head from fear and worry and pain to finding certainty, opportunity and growth.

Denial

Armed with all these ways to flip uncertainty, you should be able to find growth and a positive path forward, but you have to be able to admit the uncertainty in the first place. For some, it is easier to pretend they're not fearful. They create a delusion and pretend. For some people their reaction to the pandemic has been this thing doesn't matter, it's a joke virus, it's not real so I'm just going to carry on doing my own thing. I think we sometimes seek the answers that we want, don't we? Social media definitely tailors what we see to what we're interested in, so it makes us feel like we're right. With this, anything we say or do is supported if we look in the right places.

We might be searching for a 'new normal' that looks very similar to the comfort zone of our old normal, but one that might not actually ever happen. I'm talking about really stepping back here and saying, 'What is playing out?' It's important to stop and take a bird's-eye view of your life and look at the certainties and the things that can be controlled. Then, to look at the negative of uncertainty and think what you can actually do with it. We can all sit and plan for the future, see the uncertainty, or the effort needed to actually grow, and we retreat into our comfort zones. But what about actually doing something with that uncertainty? I think it's about saying, if we're going to do anything with our lives, let's not lie on our deathbed regretting. No one wants the eulogy at their funeral to include the words 'they just took the safe option'.

Ask any palliative care nurse to talk about what people regret most. People regret working too much. People regret not saying things that they should have said. People regret not doing the things that they know they should have done. It's the 'not doing' and 'not saying' that we regret – not the lack of comfort. We spend a great deal of our lives trying to get back in that comfort zone. And when we get knocked out of it, it's about asking that question: 'Okay, I wouldn't ask to be here, but now that I am, what can I do? What can I do to make the best of this situation? What is next?'

A cynic might suggest this is blind optimism, or naïvety, but after his experience in the prisoner-of-war camps of World War 2, Victor Frankl wrote a great book called *Man's Search for Meaning*. He witnessed the experiences of many different people who suffered and survived that most horrific of events and their outlook varied. It wasn't that survivors were overly optimistic, because that level of delusion disappointed and often crushed their spirit. It wasn't that those with a negative viewpoint were more likely to survive either, because the self-fulfilling prophecy of learned hopelessness and helplessness also broke them. Frankl commented that the people that survived were the ones that could really gain clarity on what was happening to them – not optimism or cynicism, but clarity. Frankl took his knowledge of the most terrible events humanity can inflict on itself and noticed that those who can survive these experiences create a space between stimulus and response. He says as the stimulus comes, be it grief, Covid, unemployment, the dark clouds, there needs to be a gap between the stimulus and how we respond.

This idea is developed further by Paul McGee, The SUMO Guy, who states Event + Response = Outcome (E+R=O). The time and consideration given to the response actually determines the quality of the outcome. Stepping back and flipping the uncertainty is a huge part of how you can respond to the clouds that will come. It's not as simple as learning from a negative experience, because that can certainly teach you bad things as well as good things. However, it is about using your response to get a better view of what has happened and what could happen going forward. As John Maxwell says, 'Experience is not the best teacher, evaluated experience is. . .' When you take the opportunity to evaluate those negative experiences accurately and collectively and correctly, you can see the bigger picture of the scheme of life, and you're probably better positioned to flip uncertainty negative to uncertainty positive.

Chapter 4

RETHINKING

The first three chapters of this book have hopefully provided you with a different perspective on the clouds that are arriving. Or at the very least, provided you with a few techniques to deal with the physical and mental rigours of getting knocked down. All of this is useful in helping you to find a positive way through difficult times but underlying it all is a fundamental process – and that process is decision-making.

A quick question for you: How many decisions do you think we make every single day? Hundreds? Thousands? Some of them are automatic, some of them require more time; but whatever the speed, we are making decisions all the time. Psychologists can't quite agree on the number and part of that is because it depends on what you define as a decision. Regardless of the psychologist's definition, it's said to be between 2,500 to 35,000 and that's a heck of a lot of decisions. A lot of different options that could take you down a lot of different paths. We're making multiple decisions every day and the point is that when the clouds come, you're going to be making some pretty significant decisions that are going to impact you, your life, and a lot of people around you. So how do you know you're making the right ones?

Thinking for a Change is a book written by one of my all-time favourite authors and leadership legend John Maxwell, and for me, the title is very interesting as it can work on two very distinct levels – one, that if we're going to change, we really need to think, but also, a bit more provocatively, that we really need to start thinking (for a change) because most of the time, we don't think enough. It's all about decision-making and decision management, and how we can use everything we're learning from our difficulties to think our way out of a situation with a positive outcome.

Maxwell's message is not suggesting that we're really bad at making decisions. We put a lot of time into decision-making, but we don't often then manage those decisions once they've been made. So what does that look like in real life? Well, take, for example, divorce rates. Couples make a decision, a commitment in marriage to spend the rest of their life with one another. They think about it and make the choice, but once they've made that decision, statistics show that they don't always then do a lot to manage it and the phrase 'we just grew apart' can become the new reality. With life, family and other commitments being name-checked for having got in the way of working on the relationship. But, of course, this would not have happened in the first stages of dating, so why does it happen later on, at a stage when the relationship is arguably more important?

Well, to understand this I believe we need to consider how we as humans actually think. So let's take a quick look at this. Here's a question for you: you're planning a day at the beach and decide to buy a bat and a ball to play with. The total cost of the bat and the ball is £1.10. The bat costs £1 more than the ball. How much does the ball cost?

Some of you will get the correct answer (5p), but about 80% of people will say that the ball costs 10p. It took me about two hours to understand this, genuinely, but the ball really does costs 5p, and £1 more than that means the bat costs £1.05. Confused? Look it up if you're raging at this mathematical trick. The penny will drop – pardon the pun!

I ask audiences this question all the time and like me, they very quickly jump straight in and say 10p. And the reason I use this example is because it demonstrates what Daniel Kahneman discusses in his book *Thinking, Fast and Slow*. Kahneman says that there are two ways in which we think – system one and system two. System one is what he calls fast thinking. This is quick thinking. This is intuitive. It's instinctive. This links to the Malcolm Gladwell research from *Blink*, where he talks about thin slicing. Lots of experience, lots of wisdom, lots of knowledge, all of which can help us to make very quick decisions. In a nutshell – that's fast thinking.

While fast thinking can of course be effective, and we are programmed to be able to think this way to save our energy for perhaps more laborious duties, there are many, many decisions that we have to make that require much more in-depth consideration. A decision which requires us to have to peel back the layers of the onion, weigh up the pros and cons and really deliberate. We have to really think deeply about all of the consequences, the causes and effects, problems and issues. This is system two thinking.

Kahneman says that these two decision-making systems are at play all the time. We've all had knee-jerk reactions that we reconsider with more information or a calmer head, and vice versa, we've all wished we'd reacted quicker or more instinctively in a situation that we had mulled over. What Kahneman suggests is that we need to use the right system – fast thinking or slow thinking – and we need to use

them at the right time. It doesn't sound too controversial to say this, but when the clouds come, when
we've been knocked down on our backsides, we very
often rely on fast thinking and can often fail to engage our slow-thinking process.

And when you think about it further, that's completely natural. We make thousands of decisions
each day and the majority of them do not require
the deep consideration of slow thinking. We think
fast about the majority of things we do each day:
What socks am I going to wear? Is it a Spiderman
day, or is it a Superman day? What kind of undies
am I wearing? Is it a Calvin Klein day, or is it a
Tesco's briefs day? They're fast thinking. What am
I going to have to eat now? Fast thinking. These
are not decisions that we need to deliberate over,
to weigh up options or see consequences. We can
make them quickly and it feels comfortable to do
so. You've made those choices before, so it shouldn't
slow you down, and it doesn't require a lot of brain
power. Sometimes they're even habitual.

However, there are decisions where we need to go
into that slower thinking mode, and we need to find
a way of thinking at a deeper level or higher level.
We've already talked about how our comfort zone
prevents us from dealing effectively with uncertainty. So our habitual fast thinking might need to
be challenged to help us to deal better with crises

and difficulties. How can we encourage ourselves to think slowly in these situations?

The first barrier, I would say, to slow thinking is laziness. Human beings are lazy. Not in the sense that we sit on our sofas eating doughnuts all day. I mean that our brains want us to expend as little energy as possible to function. We are hardwired to conserve energy and we use fast thinking to achieve it. Our comfort zone is comfortable because it doesn't challenge, and it doesn't make us sweat. That doesn't mean it's good for us.

Our brains physically do not like slow thinking because it uses up a lot more energy in our systems. A lot more glycogen is needed by the brain to function when slow thinking. Fast thinking is the quick and easy alternative. We also have this false idea that geniuses understand everything quickly and if the answer to a problem doesn't arrive immediately, then we must be stupid. The reality is that we discount the knowledge, experience and practice that is required by a brain to respond in a fast-thinking manner to very complex things. We don't consider the boring hard work and graft, and slow thinking that trains a brain to be able to do things at a genius level. It comes back to Dweck, who we discussed in Chapter 3, and her growth mindset versus a fixed mindset. If you know that your brain can develop and change, you will be able to help yourself make better decisions. Your decision-making can be effective and faster, but it takes some work.

The Habit of Slow Thinking – The 3Ps

So, what can we do to take people from the habit of fast thinking to the habit of slow thinking? As with the other sections of this book, we've got a process to follow. In this case, I have created a model which identifies three steps to help these ideas stick. And I call this the 3Ps: Pause, Perspective and Priorities. So what does this look like in decision-making?

Pause

The first element to go from fast thinking to effective slow thinking is the pause. The pause is powerful in all different scenarios in life. Consider a conversation where the other person isn't really saying anything. Just pause. Wait. Don't say anything. Within 15 seconds that person will respond or remark on your silence. You have literally made them talk. The pause is powerful.

Returning to our ruined picnic and the clouds arriving we can play out our two ways of thinking. Fast thinking would be getting up, grabbing the stuff and running home. You'd still get wet, you'd definitely feel stressed, and more than likely you'd be exhausted after the 100-mph dash back to the car. You've probably even lost something in the rush to clear up all your stuff and get back in the dry. Slow thinking on the other hand, would have made you look around and see if the clouds were going to pass and the blue sky return. It would help you to look for a tree to shelter under, or simply let you smile and enjoy the rain – it's not the end of the world after all. In this scenario, both decision-making processes have the consequence of you getting rained on, but the slow-thinking pause has provided a powerful opportunity to gain another perspective and allowed you to find a range of different options that you might have otherwise missed.

So why is the pause useful right now? Well, if you think about the world we're living in at the moment we've never been so contactable. If I've learned anything from all the different sectors with which I work, be it in education, sport, business, the police, or even the NHS, so many industries are expected to be constantly on. Supermarket workers didn't stop working through lockdown. Teachers were available online at times when they wouldn't normally be. People working from home were trying to juggle homeschooling and working on their laptops, sometimes at the same time. Thanks to broadband and technology, many of us remain contactable all day long. Where is the time to pause? It's no surprise that we get into quick, fast-thinking mode. We've not got time to pause. We've got texts, emails, video calls. We haven't got the walk between meetings down the corridor, the train to work, the wait at the bus stop. We're on – and on all the time!

If you are harried at all times of the day and you're still having to make all those decisions, you're going to drop the ball. It doesn't mean that you're incapable, or stupid, or failing, it just means that with that volume of decisions to be made, you might come across a decision that doesn't require a quick yes or no.

This isn't even lockdown specific. Our lives are based around convenience, accessibility and consumption. We can watch whatever we want to watch whenever we want on dozens of streaming options. We can be contacted at all times of the day within our own homes, and we expect that someone will respond. We can order food and clothes and everything we want delivered to our door, at any time of day. There is no pause. Everything is expected to be instantaneous, and we can get a little bit upset if it doesn't happen right now, and this is a real problem.

In his book *The Pause Principle,* Kevin Cashman advocates for the use of the pause. He states clearly that the power of the pause gives you so much in the simple act of stopping. One of my goals for this year, for example, is just to enjoy life more. I have lots of great things going on, but I'm always rushing to do the next thing or I'm spending too much time thinking about how I didn't like that, or how something didn't quite go as well as it could have gone. Cashman's book is the first book I read that really made me think of the tangible benefits of pausing.

A couple of years ago I spoke at the International Marketing Society event with a guy called Rob Poynton. He's a business lecturer at the Saïd Business School in Oxford and has written a book called *Do Pause*. I was fascinated by his talk at that event. I was there talking about leadership. And he was talking about the power of the pause. We went for dinner that night and entered into a great conversation about him purchasing a house out in Spain and he explained that he brings business executives over to visit and work. The moment they arrive they look around at the beautiful, calm surroundings and then with a real sense of urgency they say, 'Come on then, let's get cracking. Let's get on with work. Let's do the team build. Let's do the leadership thinking. Let's get started.' Almost immediately, they are back at that fast thinking. But instead he makes them pause. He takes them on walks. He gets them eating together. Gets them talking informally. He gets them to just be where they are. And that's when the magic happens. Away from the habit of fast thinking and fast decisions, the business leaders slow down and start being creative. The pause gives them the chance to make better, bigger, slower, more effective decisions.

Think about the number of people that have brilliant ideas in the shower or start thinking of things when they're having a walk outside. In our busy world, we rarely stop and pause. These rare moments facilitate a moment of clarity or creativity that we need to make even better decisions. It's the time when you're not chasing the idea, the ideas are coming to you. Very often in life, we're hunters. We chase, we chase, we chase. We want to get this. Come on. Come on. We're pushing, we're forcing the issue. Whereas, if you ask a fisherman what they do, they'll tell you they create an environment, prepare the space and they wait. They pause and they wait for the fish to come to them.

It's not just about pausing to give yourself a break. Resting your body and mind is a separate issue. This is actively choosing to pause because it's powerful. Pausing gets you thinking differently. I think it's the starting point for learning this habit of slow thinking. In Ryan Holiday's book, *Stillness Is the Key*, he talks about this idea of stillness – very similar to the pause. Holiday refers to many historical figures who've made really big important in-depth multifaceted multi-knock-on impact decisions. He claims that every one of them created a moment of stillness. They paused. I think it's actually when we think best, and of course the capacity for human beings to think is enormous. The capacity for human beings to be creative is utterly incredible, but we often don't have time to do it in this world we've created. What I'm saying is that in order for us to do slow thinking, we have to press pause.

It's got to be simple and it's got to be realistic. It's a slow-thinking habit that you're trying to create. I try to go for a walk. I try to sit down and have dinner with my family. If I have to do a work call, I take a walk whenever I can and get that additional fresh air. You have to try and create deliberate pause points. If you're in a meeting and it's getting to a point where you can't quite make a decision, or it's getting fractious and difficult – time to take a pause. Ask everyone to take ten minutes and stretch their legs and come back. It works. When they return, it's a different mindset, a different framework. Just ten minutes of fresh air and fresh environment – a pause. The thinking is different as a result of just taking a moment to collect your thoughts on something and find out what you really think rather than responding with fast thinking, and the feeling you've got to back it up. The first habit for slow thinking – the pause.

Not only will this pause be powerful, the pause helps us to be more present; not in the past, not in the future, but right here – right now.

Perspective(s)

Perspective is the next part of creating the habit for slow thinking. And when you think about it, it's the reason why so many people find it easier to give advice rather than to actually make their own decisions. Someone else's eyes often seem to be better than your own at seeing a situation clearly. I think that sometimes we live life really zoomed in. As if our life is only a couple of inches from the end of our nose. We can't quite see the bigger picture.

Sometimes it only takes a short conversation from a close friend to see that bigger picture and when you do, it really changes how you might make decisions. In his books *Good to Great*, *Built to Last*, *How the Mighty Fall* and *Great by Choice*, Jim Collins calls this 'zooming out'. It's the easiest thing in the world to get hung up on the smallest details, the tiniest of issues. Like the missing corkscrew in Chapter 1. Those dark clouds are on the horizon, and you lose the other possible options that you could decide upon.

I remember once I was coaching a leader and all they did was zoom in. Every time I coached them, they wanted to zoom in on just the problems and issues. Both positive and negative they were in the detail, in the minutiae, right in the thick of it and that is what made them in so many ways a great leader. But I remember taking them to the Manchester version of the London Eye – a giant Ferris wheel in the centre of the city.

We were sitting at a coffee shop in front of the wheel, and he didn't know what we were going to do, and I said, 'Tell me what you can see?' His response was to start talking about a work issue. But I kept pushing him and asking him to tell me what he could see and eventually he started to reel off a list of shops and city centre objects – 'There's Primark, I can see a bus shelter, the bus station, and I can just about see the Starbucks on the corner.' I then asked him to get up, 'Follow me!' I said, and we finished our coffee and off we went to the Ferris wheel.

At the top, the wheel usually stops and this allows you to take a photograph – an opportunity to capture the moment and at this point I asked him, 'Tell me what you can see now?' The point I was exploring earlier soon became crystal clear. He could see everything from up there. Changing the perspective was physical in this case, but it made the figurative point. Leaders cannot be zoomed in all the time. They've got to zoom out. And when the clouds come, we all need to find a way to gain some big picture perspective. Your instinct is to zoom in and you can't see the whole map, the interconnected dots, when you're so close to the issue. You just see the cause and the immediate impact. I believe we've got to think wider to make those better decisions. So, I guess it's a bit like when you're doing a jigsaw puzzle: you need to see the big picture on the front of the box when you've only got the little pieces right in front of you.

Some people get very good at pausing at these moments and finding a way to zoom out and gain a different perspective, but I'd still say that's not enough. I've put an 's' in brackets on the end of perspective in this section title for a purpose. Because I believe it is really important to get more than one. Sounds simple. But it's what the best leaders do. Our view of the world is only our view of the world. No matter how good you might be at taking a pause and gaining perspective, it's still a singular view.

To make the best decisions, you've got to gain multiple perspectives on a given situation. It doesn't mean you want consensus or that you're going to use every different view. But it will mean you have to consider a range of perspectives to make your personal decision. The best deep-thinking leaders will want 360-degree perspective from colleagues – from the CEO to the cleaner. Often it is preferable to step outside the boardroom because the ground-level employees can give you a very different perspective or advice. Those with a realistic and more grounded perspective can provide something that the top tier and hierarchy cannot.

Paul McGee talks about the beach ball effect in his work. He talks about the fact that if I put a beach ball in front of me, I'm seeing three colours. It could be white, blue and red. However, you're seeing perhaps three different colours, pink, green and yellow. But we're looking at the same beach ball. The fact is we're often going to see the same thing differently. When you're pausing, you have a chance to change perspective and that is another incredibly powerful thing. It helps us to think better, take a load off, lets us perhaps get creative.

Slow thinking is what we're after here and pausing followed by perspective(s) in a moment of difficulty is certainly the beginning. When problems arise it is very easy to catastrophise about the situation – the snowball seems bigger and bigger and looks like it could cause the end of the world, when really, it's just part of a passing snow shower. Press pause, get perspective and try to see what is actually happening. Easier said than done, but it will help you make better decisions.

It's difficult to be objective and unbiased in these situations, but the pause and perspective will give you more information and provide you with more insight. It's perfectly normal to want to rely on yourself for every source of information or advice, but whether it's pride or simply the situation that stops you asking for advice from others, it just doesn't help to be an island. Of course, you don't have to agree with the other person, or even change your mind, but the addition of another's perspective gives you depth and width and can make you see things without that same instantaneous emotional response. It's about having another alternative viewpoint. Accepting that there will be other points of view and having the strength of personality to say, 'I can still be the leader and make the right decision for me but, I need to acknowledge and understand that there will be ideas and information from other people whether they are my superiors or my subordinates.'

Now there is also the issue of timing to consider. If you've just been in a boxing match and you're on the floor having just been knocked down you're not going to be asking the audience watching the match what they think. Even though they could probably tell you – 'Well I saw what happened there. I can see why you're on the deck. You slipped, or you did this too slowly, or you've been keeping your right hand down too much. . .' Whatever it is, they will have probably seen it – but you don't ask them, because the timing of gaining perspectives will matter.

When you do ask for advice or guidance, people will be very honest with you and sometimes it stings. But you've got to work out what's happened at a low point and if the advice hurts more than the difficult situation, then you have an answer there too – maybe the situation isn't so bad. In most cases, the ego is bruised, but the advice is a learning process. The perspective is the learning bit, that helps you unlearn and relearn. I also don't think you can really get perspective unless you pause. I think you otherwise just carry on getting the perspective of fast thinking.

Priorities

Pause comes first, followed by perspective, and then what? It's now time to use the information you've gathered and set some priorities. What is it that matters most right now? Part of the feeling of panic and catastrophe is because the problem reveals a whole range of different things you might try and solve. But which first? What is our important? What is our urgent? What is our Pareto principle (the 20% of the problem that delivers 80% of our issues)?

Brian Tracy uses KWINK analysis for this very purpose. Knowing What I Now Know, or KWINK, is the first step to deciding what your priorities need to be. To make useful slow-thinking decisions, we need to see past a whole range of distractions to the key elements that matter most. This helps you decide what to do next. If the different perspectives you've been given provide you with the calm reality of your family being safe, a roof being over your head, food being on your table, you can then get to the real dilemmas. They're the things that matter most.

It is true that we can take on too much and try and do too much and therefore achieve very little or get that sense of being overwhelmed. This is one thing I sometimes see in the different areas of my leadership work; when organisations or teams are creating their strategies they will often try and achieve everything, rather than working on the most important thing(s). This overestimation of what should and could be achieved can set a team on a path to mediocrity where we only half bake our initiatives and engage with some elements that won't really make the difference.

Making the 3Ps Work for You

Going through the process of the 3Ps has helped me dramatically in my life when those difficult moments have come. It's helped me to shape my thinking and it's also helped lots of teams and lots of leaders I've coached.

A word of warning though – the 3Ps sound simple. People look at them and say, 'Got it, Drew. I need to press pause regularly to get perspective and I need to set the priorities when I've done the first two. Got it.' But it isn't actually that simple, and here's why.

With every thought process there are some pitfalls, and the 3Ps need to be viewed with a little nuance. Firstly, you have to be careful of confirmation bias. We are not unbiased individuals. When we're in that perspective section, we're not unbiased. We predict new information in line with our pre-existing views. We're not thinking, 'Well, I'm just going to look at this on the balance of face value and look at it through a fresh lens.' No, you're not. Nobody does and nobody is and it's worthwhile remembering that – that we're not unbiased.

Whenever we're getting perspective, understand that it's coming from somewhere, a place that is laid down with the foundations of all our past learnings and experiences. It is the very rare individual who could completely put everything into that objective framework and just look at this on the merits of what they're seeing in front of them. If you're one of them, then that is wonderful. But I have to admit that most of us connect to something else, so we're not unbiased.

The next pitfall to make sure you're aware of is the primacy effect. This is where we can fall in love with the first solution that comes along. The first idea is good. Let's go with this, it seems expedient and fast. It's perfectly normal – you're in a tricky situation and someone gives you an idea of how to deal with it. Boom. You throw your hands around it with great relief. You want to do that thing and quick. It changes your perspective and moves your emotions to the positive. We very often love the first idea that comes along, but it's still fast thinking. It might be right, but you need to be aware that it might not be the only solution.

It's the same too with the last thing you hear – the recency effect. Our brain likes the first and last ideas because they are the easiest and speediest to recall. If you get a group together to discuss a range of ideas – say five or six – the group will usually lean towards the first and the last ideas because of the primacy and recency effect. It suits our fast-thinking habits. It suits our need for a solution. We get an idea; we can move forward. But what about ideas 2, 3 and 4 – did they get forgotten, were they any good? I have seen this scenario play out in a number of places. The first and last idea seems overly prominent.

I was really fortunate to go on an amazing holiday a few years ago. It was an incredible holiday. It was a once in a lifetime holiday with my family. And when people ask me about that holiday, and it was utterly incredible, I have to check myself sometimes because my immediate response is, 'It was amazing, but the journey home was a nightmare.' This was a 10-day holiday in the lap of luxury, but the journey home was so long, I think it scarred me. And guess what – it was the last thing we did. The very end of the holiday. The last memory. We had to take two boat trips, three different plane journeys, with all the luggage off and putting it back on again. Checking in and out through different airports across the globe and it took about 23 hours. It was long, tiring and seemingly never ending. I'm aware of how ridiculous it sounds, but looking back at that holiday, I'm not at all recalling the amazing memories first. My residing memory – thanks to the recency effect – is this horrible feeling of sitting in airports, another bag check, and another bag check. Security checks. Laptops out. Shoes off and on. Belts off and on. In the end, I stopped taking my belt off and just played the game of Russian roulette with the security arch. Is the alarm going to go off or not? That's how hacked off I was with the whole process.

That's the recency effect and primacy effect in a nutshell. Our fast thinking makes these solutions easy. It provides us with an answer for our decision. But be aware of that, especially in meetings because we'll likely love the first idea or the last idea, and they might not be the best ideas, and these are just another two ways in which we can get hoodwinked and not quite reach that level of deep and slow thinking which might actually be best for us.

A third pitfall in this decision-making process is groupthink. It sounds very Orwellian. Images of cults, brainwashing and Big Brother may pop into your mind at this, but it's not as scary as any of that. Groupthink simply means that the first person to speak in response to an issue or an idea is key. Everyone who follows then tries to align themselves with the initial idea and speaker in some way. Or this can happen when your boss is handing over information. If the boss says something about an idea – positive or negative – most people will agree and verbally join in with that discussion. However, when the boss walks out of the meeting and the discussion or comments are reflected upon at a slower pace, they might actually reconsider the view they had just held. Like, actually that will never work, why did he/she say that, that is actually a bad idea. In the fast-thinking moment, the group has agreed on something. They've supported the person or grabbed at the primacy or recency effected idea. And this is all because, often, we align ourselves with what other people think.

You see it on social media all the time. You see the same group or crowd of people sticking together. This happens even if something opposite has been said in the past because the group has fallen into that groupthink way of thinking. Even the most independent of us can behave like a sheep in groupthink.

And our final slow-thinking pitfall is decision fatigue. About seven or eight years ago, I was doing some leadership development session work in the New Forest with a group of leaders. We were doing lots of stuff on the topics of thinking and decision-making and over dinner later that night, the delegates were merciless with me: 'I bet living with you is a joy at home, Drew. I can imagine every time you're making a family decision you get your flip chart out and you're thinking, which takeaway do we have tonight? Well, we're going to go through several thinking models to decide. . .' It was all good natured and I thought it was hilarious, but I had to admit that I'm sometimes absolutely rubbish at home. Some days I can't make any decisions on anything. I rely on everyone else to do it. After spending day after day being responsible for making decision after decision, I feel like I've had enough. My energy levels are low, and I'm just totally spent. I need someone else to sort things for me. And this is decision fatigue.

We only have a finite amount of decision-making capability per day. And that's not the thousands of simple fast-thinking decisions, but the really good, quality decision-making capability. It's something a lot of people suffer in all walks of life. You spend the day making these fast and furious decisions, big and small, and so you've got nothing left as the day goes on.

Being aware of this as you're trying to make really big decisions is so important. If you're trying to make a big call at the end of a day, be aware that the quality of your decision-making could get worse. A lot of people put meetings at the end of the day, because that's the time we have 'spare', but who doesn't feel like decision primacy or recency creeps in when you're tired? Just get it done, get it decided upon, head off home – and that's the best of us just feeling tired because it's a long day.

Now, for some people this isn't true – it comes down to something called chronotyping – some people are just better in the afternoons. My older brother's energy levels are high in the afternoon. I'm much better in the morning. So this natural effect will also have a sway too. But it's an awareness of all these pitfalls in decision-making that will help you. The 3Ps sound like the simplest of things to remember to help slow your thinking and make your decisions effective, but awareness of confirmation bias, primacy effect, recency effect, groupthink and decision fatigue are deeply important.

The 3Ps are extremely powerful and a model I have applied to a range of different industries and scenarios, from business leaders to elite sport athletes. And it doesn't always have to take a lot of time. In the sporting world, it's straightforward to think that the 3Ps can be applied after a review of a game, or in a preview of the next game. You'll play at the weekend, you'll review the last game, maybe the day after, and then you'll preview your next opponent and how you're going to play against them and then the whole week's training is based on the preview. The 3Ps are a great model for these sessions: pause, get perspective, set the priorities. But could you do it in a game? Within the moment. Applying slow thinking to a faster moving scenario – that's the dream, right?

You can't exactly stop and get a flip chart out or start having in-depth deliberations mid-game, but there is always some time to do something. Think about the moment after a try is scored, or a goal conceded, or even half-time, or breaks, you get little moments – 60 or 90 seconds, a couple of minutes – could you get everyone together? Just to pause, look around and think of what the priority should be next.

Currently in sport, a number of people are talking about nasal breathing. Breathing in through the nose affects the vagus nerve and impacts positively on the parasympathetic nervous system. It is known to help calm us down. Could you therefore do three breaths in 15–20 seconds? Could we use some seconds to quickly say what do we think's playing out here? To get a couple of perspectives pretty quickly. You have to train people into getting them to do this, but this is exactly what happens in all kinds of sports.

But why are you telling me this you might ask? We're perhaps not elite sports people, or maybe you are? Well, I'm saying this because slow thinking doesn't have to mean that it takes a long time. When I'm in a meeting and I feel I'm getting drawn into something and I'm starting to do fast thinking, I will take three nasal breaths in, which no one can see me doing. I'm not sitting in the lotus position hitting a wind chime or anything like that. I'm just taking three breaths. It can help me zoom out from the session, think about what's playing out and then I come back in and feel like I can contribute. It's a way to avoid the pitfalls. Alternatively, I might nip to the toilet. I might go and grab a coffee. And that includes virtual meetings too.

We're time pressured, but don't feel afraid to take a pause. The pause is the power play, the chance to reset. The slow thinking can be done in a very short amount of time. You can't always be Bill Gates and take 10 days away from technology on a retreat to pause your life and gain perspective. However, we can still pause, gain perspective, and prioritise in exactly the same way. Short time span, or long time horizon, we need to try and get away from the fast thinking. We need to get away from the fast thinking, in our fast-paced world and make the move to the slow thinking, and I think the 3Ps, with an awareness of the pitfalls, are the answer.

Chapter 5

DEALING WITH DIFFICULTY

The aim of this book is to provide you with advice and real techniques for dealing with difficulty, whatever those difficulties may be. But the problem with difficulty is that it will vary. Sounds obvious, but each person's difficult time is very different. However, knowing that, we've attempted to provide you with flexible techniques that you can use to face your problem head on, regardless of what it is. In this last chapter we look at the core of a difficult situation, its impact on you, and how to best get through it.

Let's start at the beginning with John Maxwell, one of the first people I read regarding difficult moments. Maxwell talks about the three stages of dealing with difficulty – stabilise, organise and mobilise. You're in the difficulty, and the first thing you need to do is steady the ship. In business or in life, just get things a little more stable and balanced. Next, try and organise things a little more, get everybody or everything back in place. And then finally, you make the move to mobilise, to do something next. Maxwell's ideas really spoke to me because of the powerful pause that doesn't just rush on in. Only fools rush in and all that stuff. Actually taking time to stabilise, get organised, look at all the pieces, then mobilise. Now, I could definitely relate to that and see how it helped dealing with a difficult moment, but I wondered if there was a little more to it.

Mountain or Molehill?

It all starts with a simple question – is this a crisis or is this a big problem? What's the difference you might ask and in everyday language, probably nothing much. But in terms of dealing with difficulty, this is the big question. Let's be honest, oftentimes in life we're throwing our hands up in the air and we're panicking, and we're scared, and we've got all the emotion we talk about and the uncertainty, and we really get ourselves in a pickle. But, when we get the chance to just take that moment and pause, we begin to see the difference between a crisis and a problem. It doesn't mean we don't feel both acutely and painfully sometimes, but there is a difference in the reality of them.

In chapter 15 of *Winners and How They Succeed* by Alastair Campbell, he talks about the first year of government alongside Tony Blair. A new government in power, a new party taking over after years of a different political regime, and Campbell refers to the media reporting he was primarily responsible for managing. He states that in the first year 'the words government and crisis turned up in headlines 202 times; in year two the figure was 376; by year four it had climbed to 418'. That's a lot of crises. But the reality, from Campbell's point of view, was that there is no way every one of those difficulties was a crisis. Maybe the foot-and-mouth epidemic was a crisis, but the rest were problems or issues at best. It isn't to diminish the problem and make it smaller, but it is to acknowledge its impact and power. It reminds me to ask the question, is this a crisis or a problem? That's a starting point. If you cannot face this question, your emotions and feelings will run away with themselves. Your thought patterns will take you down a road to catastrophic thinking. It's normal, but it's not always reality.

We're talking in general terms about cognitive behavioural therapy. More specifically, the cognitive behavioural triangle where thoughts, feelings and actions (or cognition, emotion and behaviour) play against each other to determine how we respond or think. There is an interplay between those three things and very quickly, if we're tired or we're not reading a situation objectively or we've not asked the question (crisis or problem?), we end up in more difficulty. We can easily start 'catastrophis-ing' as we've mentioned in earlier chapters and very soon our mountains grow from our molehills. So in response to this we have a thought process or model to follow. I have called this the 5H model and I believe this can help us to navigate through this struggle and work out what is crisis, what is problem and what we can do with it.

5Hs for Dealing with Difficulty

H1 – Hold Your Nerve

So, the first response to difficulty is to hold your nerve. I suppose I've learned this by being involved in sport throughout my life. I used to say that in any game, no matter what the score was, just stay in the game. Stay in the game and hold your nerve. It's a simple enough starting point but if you crumble or panic at this stage or simply give up, then the diffi-culty wins without meeting any opposition from you. Successful England rugby coach and leadership expert Sir Clive Woodward talks about TCUP – Thinking Clearly Under Pressure. TCUP was one of the big things they used when England were success-ful in their campaign to win the World Cup. The holding moment allows you to avoid the spiral and accept that the situation isn't great but not immedi-ately start jumping to judgement and calling out 'crisis'. Holding your nerve is to avoid immediately catastrophising. To stop the spiralling downwards into an emotional pit.

For me, holding your nerve is about asking the fundamental questions, 'What is happening now? Why am I feeling like this?' That's quite hard to do when you're caught up in the emotions. Referring back to our cognitive behavioural triangle – you start to get these horrible feelings, these nerves playing havoc with your thought processes and you're acting bizarrely or you're feeling terrible. What are the consequences as a result of that? What is actually happening now? We talk about being self-aware and knowing that these things are happening, but it's really hard. To be aware when holding your nerve is one thing, but then trying to self-manage that situation is another. Can you manage what you know is going on?

On a basic level it is saying or thinking: 'Yeah, I can see what's going on, but I can't do anything about it and I'm still in panic mode. I still feel like a headless chicken.' Or if I can manage to hold my nerve and self-manage: 'I know what's happening, and these are the things I've got to do. This is how I manage myself.' This process is often described like an arm wrestle with yourself – the emotions and the panic versus the self-awareness and management. It's a constant pressure, but if you hold your nerve and stay in the game you give yourself a chance to outlast the fears and come through on top.

Honesty, Humility and Hope

There are three elements to this which I first considered to be separate when I originally started to explore these ideas. However, I now believe they all fall under this overarching banner of 'hold your nerve'. The first element is about being really honest about where you are. Like, just be brutally honest. Where are you? What's really happened? Confront the brutal facts, the Jim Collins stuff. Let's be really honest about where we are right now. And I think that can really help you between going from crisis to problem. There are some things where we might say, 'It's not such a biggie.' And actually when we're really honest about it we change and realise 'No, it actually is a big deal.' Some people can downplay something that is actually quite serious. And I think being honest, just going right down into it and saying, 'What's actually happening here?' is a massive part of this process of holding your nerve.

The second element, and in all honesty, I change my mind on the order of these three components, but I think there is an element of humility that you've got to have to be really honest. If you've not parked your ego at the door and you're one of these people that says, 'I just can't take this knock.' I think it's very hard to then be honest. So, I guess there's perhaps an argument to say humility comes first. However, if you can be honest first, that can lead us to being humble next. But this is always about saying 'Well, kind of where's my play in this?' And if I was using John Maxwell's stuff from earlier, I would divide his 'stabilise' into two elements. I think you've got to stabilise yourself first before you can stabilise other people. See, you've got to work out what is really happening. And you've got to be humble as you're looking at 'This could be me'.

And this might sound crazy, but I do think it's true and it's another H, of course. I don't know why my mind works like this, but it just does. But I think to hold your nerve there's got to be an element of hope. Because if there's no hope, what have you got? People can spiral out of control with no hope on the horizon. I believe wholeheartedly in a quote from Louis Zamperini, 'To persevere, I think, is important for everybody. . . There's always an answer to everything.' And I think there'll always be a solution to whatever difficulty we are facing. Whether it's the pandemic situation that we're in at the moment, or a political upheaval like Brexit, we've just got to work out what that hope is. We might not always like every aspect of it but there's a glimmer that says we will get through it. And while we are able to say this is not ideal, this stings, it hurts, we also give ourselves that inner voice that says we will find a way through this. There is hope. This isn't going to be the end. It's not game over; we're still in the game. And those three things have helped me hold my nerve over time. Ultimately, hope is the great energiser that can give us the boost we need to find that answer.

Diffusing The Bomb

Now, interestingly, as we were doing the preparation for this section of the book, I came across a great article by Eric Barker called 'How to Be Calm Under Pressure'. Barker interviews a US Navy bomb disposal expert who uncovers three secrets to his success and my first thought was, 'Well, if you're going to learn about how to stay calm under pressure, then who better to go to than a bomb disposal expert?' Of course, in the article he says a number of things. But here are his three fundamentals. Firstly, don't get distracted by the 'what-ifs'. I thought that was really powerful. You know when you're in that difficult moment and you say to yourself, 'But what if this and what if that?' And then you catastrophise, catastrophise again and stress a little more. Well, for me this too was all about being really honest. I think this fits in with the stuff from above. We don't want to be drawn into the what-ifs. We do want to try and look at the problem objectively and clearly. Yes, that's easier written down, or easier said than done, but in a difficult situation, in a moment of being placed under pressure we must try to think objectively. Don't worry about the what-ifs of this, that and the other. Just say, 'Right, what is the issue here right now? Be honest. I'm sure we'll be able to deal with it. What do we need to do right now?'

The second thing Barker took down from the Navy Seal was that you need to be looking back at other issues from your past experiences and see if there's anything you can use. Now, when I read this, I was thinking, but wouldn't we do that automatically? And on reflection, I don't think we sometimes do. You forget that you've been through bad times in the past. And actually being able to say, 'You know what? I have been through bad times before so what did I do then? When I was on the ropes, what did I actually do?' And you mightn't have been in that exact same position before, but you can lean on the strategies and experiences you have had. It doesn't just need to be your own experiences that you lean on either, I think you can actually lean on other people and their experiences too.

Whenever I get into a particular moment that's difficult, I find myself reading loads about other people who might have been there before. People who might have been in a similar situation or worse. Trying to establish what they did – how did they respond to this? Almost feeding off the fuel of their mindset at the time. Like reading Sheryl Sandberg's book *Option B* where she talks about having that life-altering moment. What did she do? I think there's something really powerful about your own past experiences and the experiences of others. And I have read that when you reflect on how you or another person overcame an issue, it can actually serve to boost your confidence levels. What does this mean exactly? Well I guess you can feel a little bit like, 'You know what? I mightn't have been here before, with the specifics of this situation, but I've been in bad places before, and I did find an answer and that can give me the confidence to keep on going.'

For me, I wouldn't say that looking at mine or another's past experiences actually boosted my confidence levels. But I do think looking at your past experiences and someone else's can give you an uplifting hope. And I think that's a powerful aspect.

The Barker article lastly suggests: 'Emphasize the positive and focus on what you can control', and while it's perhaps an overused statement – it holds true. The Navy Seal relaying his story discusses one situation where he is literally blocked, and he can't move. The majority of his body is stuck as he's trying to get to a bomb. But he can move his hands and he can see the bomb. So, he's thinking, 'Well, I can see it and I can still use my hands'. He is focusing on what he can do, instead of what he can't, and this of course would be the third element identified. In sport, very often we talk about controlling the controllables and this is a similar concept. In those moments of difficulty, holding your nerve can mean you look at the things that you have got that layer of control over. The things that you can mould, the things that you can do. And there's usually a lot more things you can actually do than you can't do once you start to focus on this. You probably can't control the outcome, but you can certainly look at the things within your control and you can do something with that.

When I find myself in times like these, I might brainstorm the kinds of things I will do. Talk to other people, pick up the phone and have a chat with somebody who knows me and I know them. I can control that, and it really helped me to be honest, to be humble, to have hope. It has helped me. Those three things are boosted by talking.

Make a Move

Another strategy that helps me to hold my nerve is moving or changing wherever I am. If I'm stuck or I can't move forward with my ideas I grab my coat, put my shoes on and head out for a walk. Even if I'm in a meeting or I'm in a particular workplace, when discussions are becoming fractious, we can ask to pause the meeting and say, 'Let's have 10 minutes away'. I will always try and walk because I find walking helps to ground me, particularly if it's in nature. It can help us to get that early stabilisation. A chance to breathe deeply, pause and gather thoughts. It all sounds so simple and obvious, but if we don't consciously decide to do it, the busy frantic brain can dominate.

I also think when you're at work, or in your house, it might feel all small, tight and compacted and a uniquely personal frame of reference. So when you do go out into the big wide world you realise it's the big wide world. You follow a path and you'll have passed five people. And those people don't care about you, or care about what you're going through, or care about the outcome of that thing. And you could feel desperately sad about that or acknowledge that the world is a very big place and they've all got their own personal issues and struggles and how big is my problem really? I think there's a perspective-gathering from walking in nature. And while you're walking, think about the physiological changes you can make too – like focused breathing. Additionally, reading about other people who've been in difficult moments can help. Now, people may say 'What? You're in a difficult moment and you're reading misery pages or the difficult times of others – that's a bit morose.' But I would say to that, 'No. I think it helps you realise that it is not just you who might be facing tough times – that personalisation stuff.'

The final element of holding your nerve, which is really hard, and I must admit that I've only managed to do this on a couple of occasions myself, is noticing your self-talk. It's noticing the way you're explaining that thing, the difficulty, the challenge. In his book, *Learned Optimism*, Martin Seligman calls it your explanatory style. Trying to get into that internal dialogue to say, 'Where are you taking this? What are you making of this scenario?' It might be right, but of course, it might be wrong and catastrophising. So, there are lots of things to consider but that is the first element of dealing with difficulty. Hold your nerve and honesty, humility and hope are the cornerstones. Make sure you're looking as objectively as you can. Try not to get distracted nor let your thoughts run away from you. Look at the issues from your own past experiences. What did you do if you've been in some similar situation? Focus on what you 'can' do. And there's a lot you can do, even in a difficult moment. We very often think it's the end of the world and it isn't. So that, for me, is about stabilising yourself and maybe stabilising those in the immediate kind of bubble around you.

H2 – Humanise

So, the next phase of our dealing with difficulty and the next H in this process is to humanise the difficulty. In everyday life we are caught up with thinking about jobs or money or reputation or looking silly and actually we forget that life is always about people. Very often in the work context, we're talking about how can we hit the end-of-year numbers in business? How can we win that game in sport? How can we get those stats down in the police or the NHS? How do we get results up in education? How do we manage to meet some challenge or goal that is ahead of us? And we forget that in those really difficult moments, those times of difficulty, we've got to remember that life and any type of performance is about people. We've got to humanise it. So, make it about people not performance. Make it about people not profits.

I was really taken aback when I went to Jurgen Klopp's induction into the Hall of Fame. Klopp and Manchester City manager Pep Guardiola were onstage and answering questions to the great and good of world sport. I went along with a good friend who had invited me to the ceremony, and I was absolutely blown away by something that Klopp said. He was asked, in a semi-humorous way, what he wanted to be remembered for or what he wanted to be known as? And without blinking or pausing, he just said, 'A good human being'. The audience laughed thinking that this simple and powerful answer was just a joke or a gag to be followed up with a 'real' answer, but it wasn't. That was his answer, 'I want people to know me as a decent human being.' Before everything else, before the trophies, the accolades, the comments, the hero worship, he wanted to be a good and decent human. When he said that I remember thinking, 'That's actually all that matters in life.' And we forget that. When we're in that difficult moment where we might lose something, as we talked about in the uncertainty section, or we're worried about something, or we're fearful about criticism, or we're not feeling right, we forget sometimes – 'Well, I'm just a human being.'

We spend a lot of time trapped in a comparison of worth with other people around us and forget that the simplicity of being human reduces the pressure to perform. The performance is what is jeopardised by the difficulty of a problem or crisis. The humanity is sometimes what is lost. So Klopp's words rang true; actually, the most important thing is me as a human in life and those important humans around me and likewise for all of us. Business or life is all about people. People are all about relationships. And relationships are all about emotions.

It's a really simple train of thought for me. There's no point humanising your situation when you've not held your nerve because you're likely to say something ludicrous without point of focus. And this touches on the whole arena of empathy which I'm fascinated by. We can talk about emotional intelligence, but how empathetic are we, really? And how empathetic are we with ourselves? And the answer is 'not very often' in my view. A lot of research is coming out at the moment and there's some really interesting books being written about the fact that in a world where technology's growing, empathy is decreasing at the same rate. In fact, there's a group of people saying that we need to put more empathy-based things into technology. There's a big drive on this by technology companies as well. Empathy is shrinking. That idea of caring for humanity is shrinking and some people are laying that at the door of the increase in technology, which would kind of make sense. But we've got to be empathetic and we've got to understand that for ourselves.

Daniel Goleman, in his two books *Working with Emotional Intelligence* and *Emotional Intelligence – Why It Can Matter More Than IQ*, introduces us to four points within emotional intelligence. He identified step one as self-awareness. This self-awareness I think, allows us to kick-start the humanising position. We mentioned this in the section on holding your nerve. His second step is all about self-management. Just being aware of yourself while not being able to do anything about it is tough. We might think, 'Well, there is no

point to this. What's the point? I'm rubbish at that,
I know I'm doing this certain thing and it's irritating,
or I know I'm doing this and it's my down-fall and
I'm not doing anything about it.' Lots of people may
think that they understand themselves, so they
believe they are self-aware. And, they think – 'I am
managing myself' – so they are hitting the self-
management step. But there is more to emotional
intelligence than just this. Goleman gives us two
more steps: level three understanding is about the
social awareness aspect to having emotional intelligence, where we need to have understanding of the
people around us, and level four is then about the
relationship management.

And those final two elements, for me, are really,
really significant on the humanise bit. If people are
the most important thing, which I believe they are,
and it's those relationships and the power of those
relationships that really matters, then understanding not only ourselves, but other people is essential.

H3 – Hone In

The next part of dealing with difficulty is to hone
in. Once you've held your nerve, tried to steady the
ranks, started to think a bit more clearly under
pressure and you're making it about the people and
humanising the situation, well, then it's time to
hone in. Honing in is about asking a question – a

focus question. Whether we're going through diffi-culties or not, are we always aware of where our attention and focus actually are?

You might think that this an obvious question but when we're in that tumble dryer of difficulty, can we actually label where our attention is going? Is it on the right things? Is it focused on the things that can help or support us, or those around us moving for-ward? Honing in is the ability to look at ourselves during that moment and ask, 'Where is my atten-tion at during this specific moment in time?'

And this is usually followed by another rather obvi-ous but equally important second question – where do we now need to focus our attention? That's the next part in this process. We have held our nerve, humanised, and now we need to focus ourselves on where our attention is to be directed. This of course might lead to some adjustments. And this stage in the process should come with a health warning – because when you say yes to focusing on something new and claim, 'I'm going to put my attention over here', you consequently end up saying no to a list of other things. That seems blindingly obvious, but the number of times that I've been in a position where I've said, 'Well, yes, I'm now going to focus on that', and I've realised that there is a whole host of other things that I've inadvertently said no to because of that.

On this theme, someone once asked me what some of my biggest failings had been, and I thought about it for a minute and came to the conclusion that one of them would be working too much and never really switching off. Really simple. I was doing a podcast and my response to the host was, 'Well, I think not spending enough time with my family. Constantly being in work mode or thinking about work. That's one of my great regrets.' And this is because when I say yes to a certain piece of work, I'm saying no to other things and most importantly I could be saying no to my family and that is a position I would always want to improve upon. So we need to be asking ourselves, does our diary reflect our priorities?

Another great John Maxwell quote to keep in the forefront of our minds when we are trying to become more aware of this theme of honing in is this: 'What we focus on expands.' And isn't that true? We really do need to be very careful about where and what we are placing our focus on. If it is on the wrong thing, this really could magnify and shape our thoughts and ideas into things that aren't useful or helpful and this can serve to distract us.

I always ask the question, 'What matters most?' (WMM). WMM is something I remember to ask myself, and I do it in two phases normally. What matters most *now*, like immediately, as in what happens in the next 10 minutes? Or what matters most, generically, a longer-term consideration? And the reason I do that is because there is a big difference between reacting and responding and the two phases give us the opportunity to do both.

The reaction is usually more about the here and now. It's about the emotion, there's an immediacy, and very often therefore it's about the problem. So, when we say, 'What matters most now?' and sometimes I've had to do that – and in fact we all have to do that in life at times – you should ask yourself what matters most *now*, because this is the crisis moment and you've got to get through it. But remember these decisions can be based on a lot of emotion and gut feeling, which can be a good thing at the same time as being a bad thing. It can leave you obsessing over the problem. Whereas to respond, 'What matters most?', the wider question, not so tunnel-visioned is more of a response. And that can be more long term, that can often be more logical. Not always completely logical, but there's likely to be more plausible and perhaps more coherent sense brought in and less emotion than in the moment. On a logic–emotion scale, there is a definite shift and it's probably more likely to be rounded against a solution as opposed to just wondering, 'What do I do with this problem?'

I often say it's about tiny steps today, taking us towards the bigger picture of tomorrow. And sometimes you've got to react and respond. You might need to take those tiny steps today to just get you through. My favourite TV programme every year is the World's Strongest Man at Christmas time – don't judge me! And there is a challenge on this programme which is such a good representation of exactly this. If you've ever seen it, you will know that there is an event where the competitors pull some ludicrously enormous object, like a plane or disused train. They have to start off by taking those little steps because that's the only way they can overcome the inertia. To then get that real momentum going they then employ the bigger steps. And that's the key. You have to employ both, at the right time, when you're facing or coming through a really difficult time.

Thinking about the time when we make our smart decisions, it's useful to be aware of the important and urgent aspects of the situation. You may use the very familiar Eisenhower Matrix to determine the important-urgent. For anyone who hasn't come across this matrix before it is a grid of four cells that gives you a choice to place your focus relating to a decision, or task, that is either important or unimportant, urgent or non urgent. Even without having come across this matrix before you will know that we can sometimes focus ourselves on the important but unurgent stuff and this can leave us feeling like we're at least doing something about our situation. We can also get lost in the unimportant but urgent things. And if we're really feeling lost, we'll start scrabbling around in the unimportant and unurgent matters.

As you start to focus on the next question in this process of honing in, 'What are we going to do next?' I think it is really important to identify the next action/task/activity into one of those four categories of the matrix. The unimportant-unurgent is just going to be a total waste of time. Get rid of that. You can't afford to do that if you're going to focus properly. However, we often stumble on the unimportant-urgent stuff and this might be when you get hijacked by somebody responding to the difficulty with, 'You need to do this now', and you respond, 'Oh yes okay'. And you haven't considered if it's right for you now, or right at all. You just react to their urgency. It's hard to shut out that voice, but it's crucial that you do. Urgency is not always important. Urgency is not always what makes a priority.

When, of course, you finally get to the two elements that are placed to the top of the matrix, that's the bit to be focusing on. Some important stuff that's not urgent that can be postponed but not ignored. And then here is also the immediate group of tasks or activities – the important and urgent – the things we need to get onto right now to stop things from failing.

I have found that writing this down really helps and using that Eisenhower Matrix really helps me to consider, 'Right, here's 10 things I could do, which category do they go in? Where would I put those things on that grid?' I think that's a good way of doing it. I also use that as an overlay after I've had a tough day. I might look back and consider, 'How many things went in each quadrant?' So, I use it as a preview technique in a difficult moment, or even a review. Have I honed in and focused down on what really matters now or what really matters most? Honing in on these decisions is vital to help deal with that difficulty.

H4 – Habits

The next major element to consider is habits – even though this is the fourth element of the model I actually consider it to be the last, and that's because H5 requires no detailed explanation. H4, I believe, is the clincher. So let's see how far we have come. You've managed to hold your nerve, find some humanity, hone in on the things that matter most and now it's time to really move it forward. This is big. This is the chance to embed change and create a setting that deals with the difficulty and hopefully creates some pathways that avoid the same thing from happening again.

A lot of people get through the difficult moment and right away they set off – we're good to go! I've seen really successful people get through a difficulty, but then later on in their career they come up against the same problem again, so that over time they drop further and further back. It's harder to bounce back up if you don't change some of the things you do and are intent on repeating some of the errors of the past. To really get through something, you've got to create the habits at the end of it. Now, I argue that we could have introduced the concept of habits earlier on. But I think habits come at the end of our 'dealing with difficulty' process. Once you've held your nerve, made it about the people, honed in on the big stuff, then we can really create the habits that will deliver on that process.

I'm fascinated by habits and I've read about them for years. It was actually one of the first topics I read about when I began my journey into leadership. I knew that a huge part of leadership was going to be about change and that change only really comes from an accumulation of habits. People talk about big transformations; that's great. But ultimately, it'll come down to people's habitual behaviour on the back of it and whether that thing hits and sticks or falls away. For me habits are absolutely key.

Here are my top tips for habits. What are you going to make habitual? The first thing to understand is that the little things make a big difference. And I think we forget that sometimes. I'd like to link back here to the podcast I mentioned earlier and me explaining to the host that I was disappointed when I didn't spend enough time with my family. I remember once reading an article from a palliative care nurse who explained what dying people regretted the most and the big one for many people, just like for me, was working too much. It was never spending too much time with family and friends. It was never that they had laughed too much or enjoyed the world too much. And this, I have to say, got me thinking and reflecting and it was reaffirmed in my mind that actually, it is the little things that make the difference. I've been fortunate enough, so far, to be a part of what some people might say are big things: working in education, being part of a TV show, writing books, being invited to Buckingham Palace, working at Wembley in a cup final. But as great as those memories might be, I'm probably not going to be remembering these things on my deathbed. I'm going to be remembering the little things. I'm going to remember the family and the friends things. That's the stuff that's really going to stay with me and, for me, it's what matters the most.

In our busy and hectic lives we sometimes forget that. It's the little things with my kids. I can take them to lovely places, but they remember us creating Wembley in the back garden, taking a penalty shoot-out before they go off to bed and I'm absolutely terrible and they laugh at me. Or picking up the virtual reality headset and attempting to climb a wall or kill zombies and looking like an idiot in the lounge as I attack fresh air. These are the things they talk about. Each year, me and my wife Vicki ask the kids to create a list of activities that we can do as a family. And mostly the requests are pretty simple. One from this year was, 'We want to go to the cinema and to the pick-and-mix section and actually choose the biggest selection of sweets we can.' Many of these little things were taken from us in the pandemic – hugs, a pint in a pub, visiting the cinema, going to the gym – and we recognised this. We all suddenly felt the loss of those little things and we should be aware of their importance.

When we're talking about habits, we're talking about the compound effect of those little things repeated time and time again. There's a great saying amongst insurance appraisers: 'The hurricanes get all the press coverage, but termites have the biggest impact.' The tiny insignificant insects will wreck more houses than a hurricane ever will, repeatedly causing more damage and more cost.

We've all heard this stuff about tweak not transform, or tweak to transform. Very often, just little habitual shifts can make a massive difference.

Returning to the world of sport there are numerous examples of small habits being changed to bring in big results. I was once listening to an interview on the topic of golf where the expert suggested, 'You've got to adjust your way to success.' They were talking about golf specifically, saying it's a teeny little shift of hand or body or foot or grip that can make a world-class shot, or see the ball being picked out of the lake. The habits compounded, little things make a big difference and that's the first point.

The second thing to consider actually emerged from a great book by Marshall Goldsmith called *Triggers*, where it was suggested that everything in life comes from a trigger. We're triggered to do something. We think we're making conscious choices but very often we're just triggered by some-thing into taking action. For example, we might have something happen to us and so we have a ciga-rette. Or we have a tough day, so we crack open a bottle of wine, or pour a glass from the already opened bottle of wine. Or we don't stick to our diet because there's been some kind of trigger and we eat the wrong food. And it's being aware of what your triggers are for both the good and the bad.

What is the thing that triggers a good habit and what is the thing that triggers a bad habit? And very often we just aren't aware of that. So here is a reminder to ensure that we are aware of this when forming habits. That's tip number two.

Tip number three – make it easy. Oftentimes, we don't think simply enough about this. Occam's razor suggests, 'The simplest idea is often the best one.' Some people do not believe that I've trained every day for over 15 years. People look at me and say, 'You should look a lot better than that if you've trained every day for that long Drew.' And yes, that is probably true, but more often than not the response is, 'No way, how do you do it? How can you be bothered? How do you find the time?' My response to this is always very simple. 'Well, I leave my kit out, set my alarm early and never hit the snooze button.' It probably doesn't come as a surprise to hear that the reply is 'Really?' and for me there is no excuse. My kit is hanging there. If you came to our house and came to my bedroom door, you'd see my training kit right there hanging on the door handle. No excuses. I get out of bed, I walk two feet and my training kit is there, ready for me to grab. I don't need exotic training equipment because I do bodyweight exercises. There's no chance that I'm not going to do it because all I need is me and a six-foot space. Well, I'm going to have that pretty much anywhere I stay. And if I'm in a hotel – not a great vision for anyone – I don't even need kit, it's just me in my underwear using the space I have. The point is that you need to reduce the friction that prevents the good habit. This idea comes from *Summary of Atomic Habits* by James Clear, which is a book that focuses on reducing friction and making it easy to do that good thing. What are your habits that you want to create? Just make it easy. Make it simple.

The other side of this particular coin is tip number four – make it hard to do the bad things! Make it really inconvenient to do the things you might want to do that you shouldn't, or the things you find hard to stop. Some of you may remember when the indoor smoking ban came into force in the UK and how many people suddenly found it easier to stop smoking. The easy 'bad' habit became a hard and inconvenient habit because you could no longer just light up a cigarette wherever you were, you had to grab your coat and your smokes and walk outside – often in the rain and cold which was much more inconvenient. It didn't stop everyone, but the cold, rain and standing outside was enough to stop a large proportion of the casual smokers. Rightly or wrongly, the habit was changed. So, if there's something I don't want to do but can't seem to stop, I'll make it harder to do that thing. Put a lock on the cupboard with all the snacks in. Keep a timer on your meetings so you don't run over. Move the phone charger from your bedside table and leave it on the landing or elsewhere. Make it difficult to complete your bad habits.

A habit is something you automatically do – an automatic action. A routine is a series of habits in sequence. Like, for example, how you get up in the morning. You might brush your teeth first, have your shower, then get dressed before having a cup of coffee or tea. You all have your routine. But do they have any meaning to them or are they simply routines of function? They might have some purpose, but they do not bring the additional significance of a ritual. So how do you turn a habit into a ritual? According to Tanya Dalton in an article once written in *Forbes*, she discussed how a ritual is an action with meaning and rather than just talking about habits and routines, part of dealing with difficulty is to actually start to create rituals.

Looking at my own routines and habits I started to ask myself 'so what do I get from my training'? What's the meaning behind it because I don't ever really want to do it. I never wake up and think, yes, I'm training this morning. In fact on some days I actually feel like I'd rather boil a part of my body than do it. But I make myself do it because I think about the outcome as opposed to the process and I know that after it I'll feel great. I'll feel energised. It will clear my head. It will get me thinking better. It will allow me to do my job better. That's a major part of it. And then I started looking at what I was listening to while I exercised or walked or ran, or when I was commuting, and I made a conscious decision that I was going to listen to leadership material and do my own learning in these circumstances. This again was a conscious decision because I thought that it would really help me to get perspective and get my brain in gear. And do you know what? It's one of the best things I've ever done. Walking around London, earphones in, or walking the dog at home, I'm listening to something. I'm getting perspective on life because I'm outside. And boom, that's where my best ideas come from. This is my habit and my routine with meaning. It's now become my ritual.

This is an incredibly personal part of the process. Too many 'experts' will advise following the rituals of highly successful people – anything from Bill Gates's sleeping habits, to a celebrity's meal times, but the routines you change into rituals must be yours and must have meaning for you. They have to stick, and they have to help you to move forward. Not everyone gave up smoking by being sent outdoors – so that ritual or habit change didn't quite stick.

The final element of habits concerns this: what gets measured – gets done! To keep on track, you've got to keep track. So, if you want to create something you need to have a tracker of some description, for your own sense of accountability and achievement. You'll see this very often in journals and habit trackers. Anyone I work with, I ask them what they want to do and then suggest they create the habits to achieve this that they can then track. At the end of the day, tick it off. You do not want to go to that board and put a cross. No one does. We just don't like doing it. So, track it. To keep on track you have to be tracking it.

In short, we are all creatures of habit. But I'm not sure how strategic we are about them. I think sometimes we don't choose our habits and our habits choose us. We fall into patterns of behaviour based on our triggers – good or bad – and creating the good habits gives us more control and enables us to be better prepared and more able to recover when things get difficult.

Habits are a huge part of the moving forward process after the clouds come. It's the little things that will make a big difference, so be at peace with that. Adjust your way to success. Consider what are your triggers. Be aware of the things that you want to do and the things you don't want to do. Make it easy by reducing the friction. Make it hard and remove the temptation. Create the rituals that give meaning to your habits and understand the purpose behind that thing. And finally, what gets measured gets done. If you have a scorecard for that thing, you won't go far wrong.

H5 – The Final H

When dealing with difficulty we have to focus on the four main elements we have just covered: hold your nerve, humanise, hone in, and create habits. This is the model for dealing with those situations. A model that has been used many times with people that I've worked with specifically when they're dealing with the bad stuff. And in all seriousness, it's the reason for this book. Whether the difficulty is life threatening or not, the effect can be huge on the individual at the heart of it. Advice is all very well but having a framework to work on can be a wonderful way to move forward. Despite all of this, I had the nagging feeling that something was missing from the model. Every time I had used this framework, I was both happy that it helped, but irritated that something felt like it was still missing. Then, I realised what that missing element was. It was humour. Now that may seem strange when exploring the processes for dealing with difficulty but the importance of humour when the clouds come is unquestionably human.

Steve Rizzo, a comedian in America who does a lot of leadership talks always says, 'We're not human beings, we're humour beings.' Now I realise that this sounds like it's got about 20 layers of cheese on it, but I think there is some real truth behind it. Humour can help to get us through those difficult moments. Laughing at yourself or at the ridiculousness of the circumstances, or the interactions with people. That laughing moment – a massive, massive antidote to a wave of stress and anxiety that's coming over you. It's not easy to do, but finding something and laughing at it, well it can be good therapy. It can be a great medicine for a difficult moment.

Why the 5Hs?

I use the word 'moment' a lot and it seems relevant when talking about humour because doing what I now do, I observe people and the way people talk a lot. The more and more you hear people talking about crisis or personal or leadership challenges, they often talk about 'moments' – 'Yes, we're in a difficult moment' or 'We had a good moment'. I used to be quite critical and didn't really get it – 'What you on about?' But then I read the book *Moments* by Chip and Dan Heath and loved it. The more I looked at this idea, the more I came to the realisation that life is a collection of moments. And each of these moments can either see you fly or see you fall. They can see you sink or sail. These moments are really big to you. And it's what we do in these singular moments that matters.

Dealing with difficulty hangs upon a moment and I created the 5Hs to help people in their moment of dilemma and struggle. To overlap John Maxwell's 'stabilise, organise, mobilise' and enable everyone to process and build after these moments. 'Stabilise' becomes Holding the nerve, which enables you to Humanise and Hone in and 'organise' yourself ready to create the Habits that 'mobilise' and move you forward. The Humour keeps the soul and mind focused in the most difficult times and provides that relief and levity when all else seems dark.

I was reading Ross Edgley's book, *The Art of Resilience*, and in chapter 11 he talks about ways in which we process pain. He admits he has done some wacky things; one of them, which nobody said was possible, was that he swam around the coast of the United Kingdom. He talks about how humour kicked in as a response to pain. And I found myself completely agreeing with him. In the most painful moments of life, I have found some dark reasons to laugh. Laughing at my stupidity. Laughing at the unfairness of it all. Laughing at behaviours that in a moment of clarity just seem foolish. It gets you through. Humour provides a release, or a perspective, or a place to release emotion, or as he calls it, 'Humour is an adaptive coping mechanism for pain.'

And I suppose we have all seen some of that, haven't we? For example, there's a lot of laughter in hospices and care clinics. They're not what you think when you go there. I remember once visiting one and I saw lots of smiles and fun and laughter and I was thinking, 'Well, I wouldn't have expected this from a palliative place of care.' I know that when friends of mine have been coming towards the end of their life, the people who've been there with them in their most difficult of moments have found the strength to have a laugh and a joke, even right at the end. Or it's the bit at the funeral where someone's giving a eulogy and there's a funny comment and some funny reminiscing and there's laughter. It just makes that moment better sometimes, doesn't it? There is something about it that's like an anaesthetic in some way. A laugh can be shared. A positive moment in an overwhelmingly negative situation. It's not that you are laughing at the tragedy, but the laughter can make the tragedy seem more bearable. The laughter gives you an energy or perspective to take on the next challenge, when you thought you just couldn't make it.

And if nothing else, humour is a great way to help you find humility as a human or leader. The first thing that is clear when you're laughing at a situation or yourself, is the humility. If you can't laugh, then it means you've put the ego first and that's one of the first things you need to get rid of. The sort of celebrities we love the most aren't the ones who take themselves the most seriously, they're the ones that take the mickey out of themselves and send themselves up. They're the ones that know that fame is ridiculous and know the celebrity situation is ridiculous. Knowing that life is ridiculous in many ways, well, it helps to get you through. The ego keeps you embedded in the negative emotions surrounding the problem. The humour provides relief and a way into the positive, however dark it may seem.

These 5Hs have been around in my brain for a long time. In fact they've literally been printed, laminated and stuck up on the walls in my office for years. It's been a process of reading, a note taken, an idea added, and I've used it myself when I've faced those difficult times. Back when I was a head-teacher and the GCSE results were coming in and I expected that they weren't going to be great, I would look at these ideas, this model, and it would really help. I held my nerve and tried to think clearly. I tried to focus on the pupils and teachers – the humans involved – not the job or the other outcomes. Then I had to respond somehow. We could have done a million things differently in response, but not all of them were good ideas. We had to hone in and choose what to do next. Then I had to consider what next and what habits to build up for the future. And throughout it all, I spent a lot of time laughing at the ridiculousness of the situation, and of me, and of some of the other elements of my role that made life difficult. Not to dismiss the seriousness of it all, but to ensure I could deal with it. To ensure I could move forward positively. So I was probably the first guinea pig for the 5Hs. The first leader to use this leadership framework. And I've shared it with so many leaders over the years since and it really helps. So my hope is that now it can also help you with whatever you are facing, or may in the future face.

The Top 10 to Take Away from *When The Clouds Come*

Your top 10 tools to come back bigger, better and not in bits! And a quick way to reference.

1. Remember your ABCs – Always Be Curious
    The simple, easy, ever-present and essential questions include: Why did that happen? Why did we do that? What could that mean? Find these and many other questions from Chapter 1 onwards.

2. It's all about the growth – mindset, perspective and thinking with a future focus
    Growth is far more important than goals. You can hit a goal and not perform well. . .and miss a goal but be brilliant. Growth is the true indicator of success and lasts a lot longer. It's the science and art of resilience in Chapter 1.

3. Be a realistic optimist – confront the unknown, pragmatically and positively

   This message comes up regularly throughout the book. Both Drew and Sam firmly believe you have to be honest, face issues head on, and that better times will come. It's one of the reasons this book exists. You'll find out more in Chapter 2.

4. Life's a team sport – who's in your team?

   We are not alone. We don't need to and shouldn't want to 'do life' without those key players around us. Their offer of support, alternative perspective and laughter in the face of dark clouds can really help to push (or pull) us through.

5. Courage demands a sprint and a marathon!

   Chapter 2 takes on the mighty theme of courage. How we need to think smarter and more slowly before we start on the way forward after the storm has hit.

6. To really listen allows you to really learn – which voices are you hearing?

   In times of trouble it can be difficult to hear the useful information coming your way. Positive self-talk and an understanding of how your internal dialogue is working, along with listening to those on your personal dream team, can really help to ease uncertainty.

7. Opportunities or obstacles – what do you see?

   It's hard to find a way through when we are faced with adversity and uncertainty – see Chapter 3. But we can take a deep breath and choose the mindset we need to adopt. Look for the opportunity, see a path forward and try new things. The alternative – we become stuck in what we can't do and keep bumping into the barriers of the way we used to do it.

8. Press pause for peak performance

   Chapter 4 is not about the quick think, or the fast decision. Instead it's about the power of pausing, slowing down to go faster. Slowing down to achieve that holy grail of peak performance.

9. Be aware of brain bias

   Do we ever actually realise just how biased we as humans can be? We talk about confirmation bias, the primacy and recency effect, groupthink and lots more in Chapter 5.

10. Don't drop your Hs when tough times are here.

   Chapter 5 explores the model for finding your feet and flourishing in difficult moments. Take the 5Hs and find a way back to happiness.

Meet the Authors

Sam and Drew's Final Words

When the Clouds Come *is the first book that Sam and Drew have collaborated on, and in the introduction they explore their reasons for writing it, but they thought it might be interesting to finish off with a chance to get to know them and what brought them together. A few days after the final draft was submitted, they sat down for a cup of coffee and a chat – here's the transcript of their conversation:*

DREW: Well, we're all finished, and this is the last chapter. You and I have got to know each other over the last couple of years, become mates, but I know you well and it wouldn't be enough just because you knew somebody, or you were mates with them, that you would actually want to do a book. So, what was it for you that made you think: 'Actually, there might be something in this. I think I can work with this crank?'

SAM: Well, I wouldn't say crank at all. That's the thing, I think it was very surreal when you like wandered into my house and I'd seen you on TV and you're there. It's like – that's really weird. It's the guy off of the TV.

DREW: If memory served, you actually said to me, 'I thought you'd be a lot taller.'

SAM: Yeah. Exactly. Straight away. But I watched all the *Educating Manchester* stuff so I kind of knew what I felt about that guy. You. In most cases, I'm on the side of the educators because I've been a teacher for 17 years. So, for me, that was part of it. But it was really nice to meet you and just talk about things because obviously when I'm talking about teaching, and I naturally do talk about education in general, it's always about people. It's not necessarily just about curriculums and models and all that kind of stuff. I've always looked at it kind of holistically. I think when you were talking about anything, it was very people-based. We both kind of met at a point where I think teaching was part of what we'd done and we're kind of professionally proud of and known for, but I also think we'd also stepped into different roles now.

  You were stepping into a different role with your business and it's much more about how leadership works. A continuation of themes of what you'd already been interested in, but it definitely pushed forward after the Harrop stuff. I was three or four years into being mainly a stay-at-home dad and doing what all that involves, as well as doing my London Bookman stuff and it felt like we were on the same page. I think I was actually relatively quiet when you first came to the house because I always do this thing where I listen if I'm unsure – I'll let you talk first and then see what happens.

DREW: Yeah. There was an interesting crossover though with the people thing because I've been saying this, what I saw top level coaches do was the same as what I saw teachers do, which is what I saw great leaders do in business and great leaders in the police and in the NHS. There's definitely something there that we found a very common ground. People can be brilliant and that was the thread. I think that kind of got us on the same page, this belief that people can do, and people can be a lot more than they probably realise.

SAM: Absolutely, the realistic optimist that you mention in the book – that was the connection. I've said words around that fact for years since I've been teaching. I'm a cynical old thing, but I don't want kids to be cynical because cynicism blinkers the world and that's rubbish. For me, it's combining cynicism, knowing that things can be rubbish and people can be rubbish and things can go wrong and all this kind of stuff that's negative, but still. That's why I have always been passionate about books. Books have always had the hope thing. I'm a big, big hope person. I might grumble, I might groan, I might be critical, I might scream and shout at the negativity of things and things that don't do it, but I'm essentially, I'm wanting things to go well for people.

I think we both clicked into that. We're both realistic optimists, maybe from a different sort of direction, but I think it just clicked. I'm backward in coming forward to be honest. You're very much more: I've got my plan, I'm going to do this, I'm going to try and do this and this, etc. You have a dynamism which I absolutely admire, and I will be stimulated by that. I'm stimulated by people who have got more energy than I have. It's inspiring.

DREW: It was a strange thing though, in terms of the fit for this project because, if I think back. . .I think I mentioned it once to you, just to gauge what your thoughts on it were because we'd had some great conversations. Then, suddenly, it just all kind of fit into place. And perhaps that was the moment where you thought it might be a good idea to collaborate?

SAM: Well, I think you'd already worked out the stuff you wanted to do as a person, but I also understood *why* you wanted to write this book. I didn't even question that. I didn't question your motives in the choices you made. For me, that's very important. I might not myself have gone – well, I'm going to write this book about leadership and difficulties because it wouldn't necessarily have occurred to me that anyone would want to hear what I had to say. But you and I were listening to one another, and we were talking about it and suddenly, there's an idea there. I wanted to help make this thing happen. I could see you had all these ideas that you wanted to put into one place. I could see your purpose. I could see how that was going to work and I wanted to make it happen. I mean, what's was your drive for doing the book with me do you think?

DREW: Well, if I'm honest I've come to the realisation that I very rarely like to do things on my own. I think if I'm going to do it with someone else, it's just going to be better.

I know I'm not very good at many things. I'm really not. I've got a very narrow skillset and I'm comfortable with that. I know if I'm going to do something like a book that I'm dyslexic. I don't read a lot – as in actual books – because I find that difficult, so instead, I listen to a lot of audio books. I'm going to struggle with that process alone because I find reading and writing intensely difficult. I also believed you were going to make it better. It was that simple for me. I knew from the discussions we were having and the questions you asked, you were stimulating my thinking too. For me, the fit just seemed absolutely right. Of course, I was delighted when you finally agreed that you would do it – so thank you for that.

SAM: Yeah. That was it. It felt very natural. It does help that we both want to talk. We're both chatty buggers. You came at a time when there were difficulties for you, so it seemed like it was a natural process. Watching your ideas unfold. I remember you saying, 'Well, I've read this thing that in my experience works like that, and I think I could add things to this', and you were interestingly doing what I think the best coaching or training does. The best training that I've ever had doesn't just show you a bright new shiny thing that you've never seen before. It also confirms what you thought you might have already known or had a gut instinct for. Maybe puts a label on top of it, and then maybe takes the next step of pushing you along to – where's this going, what can we do with it, how can we do something to help others with it? To me, that's where your thinking went. And actually, when I was trying to change from a journalist to a teacher, I looked for connections like you do, looked for connections that make sense and things that then compel you forward in some ways. Your thought processes were like that. Much better planned, much better organised, much more controlled, but I could see my mind worked quite like yours.

I also think writing the book like we did, recording our conversation and listening to what you had to say and then working around it and working on it, for me, it felt like we could push something into that next space quite nicely. There's a third space that you talk about in the book, not Starbucks as you mention, but between you and me which is where the book exists, where your brain and then some of our thoughts kind of combine to something. For me, that's the metaphor of our process. And fundamentally, it's been fun. It's been a pleasure because it's just, well, it's just interesting.

DREW: I mean, in terms of the process, I think it's worked well. That idea of us talking about things, collating it then re-editing it down. It seemed to me like a really good way to do a book. Well, it worked for me anyway.

SAM: Yeah, definitely. And in terms of why you wanted to write a book in this particular area, at this particular time, why do you think the time is right now, for you?

DREW: I think it was probably a number of things that collided. It's been a topic I've been interested in for years. I've written about it. Brilliance and high achieving in all areas is something to learn from, but it can be difficult to do anything other than admire it, or try to replicate it. Difficulty is something different. So, how is that relative to me and how does that relate to me? Well, we all go through difficult times and that's the bit that I found fascinating and have done for a number of years, and I've spoken about, and I've collated things over time and tried things with leaders.

Some of those things haven't worked and some things have worked. I think what brought it into really sharp focus was the COVID-19 pandemic, that crisis I think, where I was working with individual leaders and teams. You were seeing difficulty on the news. We all felt that moment of – how are we going to deal with this? How do we process this, how do we position this, how do we get perspective on this? The more I was doing, the more I was realising that the stuff I'd been through was actually a great training ground for me to be able to deal with the issues that were quickly arising and helping other businesses and people through that. It was that thought process that made me go – do you know what, this stuff's working. It's helped me and my family. It's helped loads of leaders. We can be assured that bad times are going to come. Adversity is going to come towards us. We know that, but what do we do?

And picking up on the positive psychology stuff. I've been fascinated for about 15 years reading around that subject. We know a lot about what happens when the brain doesn't work well. We know more and more about Alzheimer's. We know about dementia. We know about depression. We know a lot about what happens when the brain doesn't work as it once did. But what happens when the brain does work well? How do people deal with difficulties? How do some people work to post-traumatic growth, and others fall prey to PTSD? Why is it that some people are able to grow through difficult times and some people won't? There has to be some kind of mental model that can help people during this time to be pushed towards more positive outcomes. I think a few things collided together. My aspirations in that area have always been to help people with difficult moments.

Again, I'm certainly not saying I've had the most difficult life because I haven't. But when those difficult times come, what mode do we go into? Very often, we just flip into automatic pilot mode and it can take over us and put us in a really bad place. Is there a way that we could look at things and certain patterns we could follow and almost retrain our brain to think, 'Okay, so this has happened. What do we do now?' I hope that this book can help with that. Where people can pull out the book and perhaps read a chapter on, for example, being more resilient – or maybe decision-making when they are in that storm.

SAM: I'm interested as well because our friendship, and subsequently putting this together, did come off the back of some difficulties. Imagine a road less travelled – if things hadn't ended in the way they did at the school, do you think this book would have even happened? I know it's not the only difficulty you've been through. I know it's not the only thing that you've had to face that has been tough; like you said, we've both had very good lives, but we've also had some other bits that aren't so good.

DREW: I think it would. I really do. Because when I reflect on the whole situation of my career and I have to say that, okay, some difficult stuff happened, but that happens to lots of people as we discuss in the book. I think it's looking at it and saying – no, there are so many successes, too. There are so many great experiences that you can't forget. You can't allow the difficult times to block out all the good things. And actually, it wasn't just the ending that was difficult. It was lots of things. Dealing with the financial challenges that the school had and being told – well, no one can do this. You won't be able to do that. It was lots of stuff that people in this position are facing. There are people who get in touch with me who are leaders who are absolutely 100 miles an hour doing great things, pulling up trees – as we say up north, doing a great job. But there are also loads of people who get in touch because they are having a tough time. It was that,

I suppose, that's compelled me to be interested in doing it. Not just for me, because if it was just for me, I probably wouldn't bother writing a book.

SAM: Yeah. I think the way you dealt with what was happening when you left the school and where you and I connected over some of that, in a way, is what made me want to write a book with you about difficulties. For me, it was how you dealt with it. Dealt with the difficulties of that, and the positivity of it that I admired. It is the realistic optimism in everything you did at that time. I really think you demonstrated some of the things that a human being can do in response to difficulties, good, bad or otherwise. I think when we look at this book that we've put together, and ask how is this going to be helpful? This is about actually, this rough stuff happens. And like it has with you, bad stuff has also happened for me and now we've been through it we can say this is what we've learned, and this is what we can put forward and this is what we can help others with. I definitely don't think your ending at Harrop is the defining moment of you, but you've been able to look back and say – well, this is what I learned. There you go world. This is how I can use that to now try and assist and help others who may also be having a tough time.

DREW: Yeah. Yeah, it absolutely makes sense. Of course, you and I would never have met actually if that hadn't happened. A massive part of this is giving people the optimism and hope that they can get through those difficult times as well. Because it's okay saying, 'This will work. This will work. Try this', because people will naturally respond with, 'Well, how do you know? How do you know it'll work?' And, well, I know it'll work because I've used it personally for myself, with friends, family, colleagues, and with a whole host of other leaders that I feel really privileged to have worked with. I think that is a crucial aspect to it. A lot of these things had been written, some part written, way before the ending at Harrop. But, like with anything, have been recrafted and refined without a doubt since then.

SAM: That's the thing, I think another one of the reasons why we connected and I wanted to be part of this is because actually, there's a sincerity within you that I definitely saw and was like – well, this guy's not full of nonsense. He's backing up everything he says and with proper expertise and knowledge. It's not just – I think this and I'm going to guru it. That's where I'm sort of sceptical of the world. Not in the human's ability to be brilliant and wonderful and kind and hopeful and optimistic. But in my realism, is that I think a lot of people will do a lot of things for nonsense reasons. I didn't really think about it much before meeting you to be honest. When you came in the house, I was like, 'Well, you're in my house. I'll listen to what you have to say.' But automatically, my brain's going, 'Is he talking nonsense or not? Is this real?' And the more and more I got to know you, the more I knew you're absolutely 100% real. That's what the brilliant thing is and that's what my compulsion to write with you is. The knowledge that we've got something here that's real, and it's smart, and it's thought through, and it's revolutionary without trying to reinvent the world.

DREW: It's an interesting point that though. Probably, if you hadn't I don't think I'd have done it either. I think when two people meet and you just feel the fit's right. That's one of the things I'm interested in from a leadership point of view. Can this team work together? It's very much like the work I do in sport. It's making sure the fit's right. The fit just felt right from our early conversations, meeting, sharing a beer together.

So, talking of difficulties – what would you say then the most difficult part of it's been? You can be honest because I know you will be anyway, but I'm not the easiest person to work with. I know that.

SAM: No, in all honesty, it's been that balancing act because I'm not a full-timer especially when I'm looking after my kids. That's the bit that I found most difficult. Working out time to discuss and write. Fitting it in around child-care, life in general and your work life. That's been interesting – carving that space out. I felt it was important to make sure that the book still sounds like you and it doesn't turn into some boring preachy self-help nonsense that doesn't really register with people. There's something about when people sit down and chat with us, they get some sincere, intelligent bits of advice and experience that will help them. We're here to help, but not in a horrible, we know better, kind of way. Here's 10 things that could help – take what you need.

DREW: So, have you yourself been through any tough times, and if you have, do you think this book would have helped you?

SAM: I think, yeah, definitely, career-wise. Education is one of these jobs where the highs are incredibly high and you witness children doing things that they couldn't possibly imagine themselves doing, and they do it and then they go beyond that, and they become these wonderful people. And then you see the lows. You see the horrible difficult things that happen there. Yeah, I've been through some horrible things within education – mainly with adults. Like everyone else, bad managers and leaders who pretend to want to support the development of young people, but actually patronise and foster low aspiration. It was hard to take sometimes. There have been clashes of personality and, sometimes, I've come off badly in that situation in terms of how emotionally broken down I've felt by things within systems and schools.

That was why a lot of the things that we wrote about in the book resonated with me. I think it's helped me process some of the things I didn't do as quickly at the time. I think it's going back and realising I got there in the end. I paused eventually and I worked out what was a response rather than a reaction. But I did react first, and I did stay with the emotion first, and I did repeat the same processes, and I got back up and tried to do the same thing over and over again before I turned tail and went – look over here. This book explores processes that would have taken me six months to a year to resolve by myself. So, if I'd read the book that we've written, I might have got there quicker. I might have got there without so many black clouds lingering over my head.

Once you can process these things, you can get yourself in that position where you can look at an emotive dark problem in a different way. It's about whatever your moment of difficulty is, these are the things that might help you process through them. I think it definitely puts a framework on things that I'd already thought through myself. It gives me a list of things I could go through that are firm and contribute to what I was already trying to deal with.

DREW: Well, that's amazing and I love that! And that for sure is what I hoped it would do and what it could be like. And now then – what's your biggest hope with this book in terms of how it will be used?

SAM: I think very much like you said before, I hope people will use it and it will really help. I haven't got visions of it being on bookshelves in any particular people's offices or anything like that, but I'd hope people would read it and go, 'Yeah, that makes sense. That would help if I can remember that, yeah. Take a deep breath at a moment of difficulty and reflect back on what that book has said or that book has in it and refer to it.' So, use, I think, is my simple definition. I want people to use it.

DREW: I think I'm the same as you. I'm hoping it's going to be a must-read for anybody facing a tough time. I hope that everyone can access it. Read it and reframe things. I suppose for me, I was trying to capture what would be as useful to as many people as possible, because very often books are targeted towards a particular audience. I'd like to think that this wasn't as targeted and that people of any age, of any work role (or not) could pick up the book and take something from it. Whatever you were going through, however experienced or inexperienced you were in life, there'd be something in it for you that would positively impact your life.

SAM: I think we could have gone into a lot more detail about the science and the cognitive ability of the brain stuff and how it functions physiologically and psychologically, and we could have gone into much more depth and create a very different book of scientific merit in some way. We could have even gone down a route for much more of an educational purpose, like teachers using this in the classroom to deal with difficulties and you become behaviour management gurus. But that wasn't what we wanted to create. I think we've both wanted some useful practical general advice for people. How do you specifically target someone's difficulty if you don't know what it is? That's where this book is a conversation. Because what we're trying to do is clear – if you have a difficulty, we don't know the depth of your feeling for that difficulty. For me, it's about that. What is the advice and what is the guidance and what is the help and the usefulness when we don't know what the cloud is?

DREW: I like the cloud analogy because it can be a really sunny day and then a cloud can just come. It can stay for 30 seconds, and it can just be just slightly irritating or it can be a welcome break actually, you didn't know that you needed to have. Whereas it can also be a huge thunderstorm. It can be lightning. It can be all of that. Clouds can come in various sizes and that's, I suppose, what happens in life. I don't know. I'm very excited about the future, and I'm also aware that bad times are going to happen, as they do for everyone. I feel I'm the best prepared I'd be in my life to face whatever comes my way. I don't know what's around the corner. No one knows. But I think I'm better prepared, and I think my family's better prepared to go through that. I'm sure there'll be lots of great stuff on the way too, and I work very hard to try and make that become a reality.

Bibliography

Barker, E. (2017). How to be calm under pressure: Three secrets from a bomb disposal expert. *Observer* (2 February).

Campbell, A. (2015). *Winners and How They Succeed.* Pegasus.

Cashman K. (2012). *The Pause Principle: Step Back to Lead Forward.* Berrett-Koehler.

Clear, J. (2018). *Atomic Habits, Tiny Changes Remarkable Results, an Easy and Proven Way to Break Good Habits and Break Bad Ones.* Avery/Random House.

Clear, J. (2018). *Build Good Habits and Break Bad Ones.* Cornerstone/Random House.

Collins, J. (2001). *Good to Great.* Cornerstone/Random House.

Collins, J. (2009). *How the Mighty Fall and Why Some Companies Never Give In.* HarperCollins.

Collins, J. & Porras, J. (2004). *Built to Last: Successful Habits of Visionary Companies.* (2004), Harper Business.

Dweck, C.S. (2007). *Mindset: The New Psychology of Success. How We Can Learn to Fulfil Our Potential.* Ballantine.

Edgley, R. (2021). *The Art of Resilience – Strategies For An Unbreakable Mind And Body.* HarperCollins.

Everly, G.S. Jr., Strouse, D.A. & McCormack, D.K. (2015). *Stronger: Develop the Resilience You Need to Succeed.* AMACOM.

Ferriss, T. (2016). *The Tools of Titans: The Tactics, Routines, and Habits of Billionaires, Icons, and World-Class Performers.* Vermillion.

Fields, J. (2012). *Uncertainty: Turning Fear and Doubt into Fuel for Brilliance.* Portfolio.

Frankl, V.E. (2011). *Man's Search for Meaning.* Ebury Publishing/Rider & Co.

Hansen, M.T. & Collins, J. (2011). *Great by Choice.* Cornerstone/Random House.

Heath, C. & Heath, D. (2017). *The Power of Moments: Why Certain Experiences Have Extraordinary Impact.* Bantam Press.

Holiday, R. (2020). *Stillness Is the Key.* Profile Books.

Gladwell, M. (2007). *Blink: The Power of Thinking Without Thinking.* Back Bay Books.

Goldsmith, M. (2015). *Triggers. Creating Behavior Change that Lasts. Becoming the Person You Want to Be.* Crown Business/Currency.

Goleman, D. (2005). *Working with Emotional Intelligence.* Bantam.

Goleman, D. (2005). *Emotional Intelligence: Why It Can Matter More Than IQ.* Random House (10th Anniversary edition).

Kahneman D. (2013). *Thinking, Fast and Slow.* Farrar Straus & Giroux.

Maxwell, J.C. (2005). *Thinking for a Change: 11 Ways Highly Successful People Approach Life and Work.* Centre Street/Faithwords.

Maxwell, J.C. (2007). *Failing Forward, Turning Mistakes into Stepping Stones for Success.* Nelson Business/ HarperCollins.

McGee, P. (2015). *S.U.M.O (Shut Up, Move On): The Straight-Talking Guide to Creating and Enjoying a Brilliant Life.* Capstone.

Poynton, R. (2019). *Do Pause: You Are Not a To Do List.* The Do Book Company.

Quoidbach, J., Gruber, J., Mikolajczac, M., Kogan, A., Kotsou, I. & Norton, M.I. (2014). 'Emodiversity and The Emotional Ecosystem'. *Journal of Experimental Psychology General,* 143(6): 2057–66.

Sandberg, S. & Grant, A. (2019). *Option B: Facing Adversity, Building Resilience and Finding Joy.* Ebury Publishing/ WH Allen.

Seligman, M.E.P. (2018). *Learned Optimism: How to Change Your Mind and Your Life.* John Murray Press/ Nicholas Brealey.

Syed, M. (2016). *Black Box Thinking: Marginal Gains and the Secrets to High Performance.* John Murray Press.

Tracy, B. (2011). *Eat that Frog! The Power of Self-Discipline.* Vanguard Press.

Tracy, B. (2012). *No Excuses! 21 Great Ways to Stop Procrastinating and Get More Done in Less Time.* MJF Books.

Treasurer, B. (2019). *Courage Goes to Work: How to Build Backbones, Boost Performance, and Get Results.* Berrett-Koehler Publishers (10th anniversary edition).

Index